Fall in Love with Your Life

SEASONAL PLANNER

This planner belongs to: _____

Date: _____

Fall in Love with Your Life
SEASONAL PLANNER

A Heart-Centered Feminine Way
to Organize Your Time

EMILY MADILL

A weekly planning ritual using the

Fall in Love With Your Life

SEASONAL PLANNER

To order more planners visit emilymadill.com

Welcome

When we fall in love, everything makes us smile. We seem to glide through life and wake up excited to greet the day. You can get that same kind of glad heart feeling for YOUR life — by design.

Hi, I'm Emily Madill I've been using variations of this planner every week since 2017. As an author and entrepreneur, a full-time mom, coach, business owner, and wife, I've tried lots of methods and tools to move toward my goals without burning out.

From childhood, I've always loved stationary and creating lists. Through university and into adulthood, I used a paper planner.

Putting pen to paper has always helped me glide through life. Looking back now, it's no surprise I've chosen to take on the path of a writer. To this day, I start every article with pen and paper. Funny enough, I also married into the office supply industry. Our family business is a locally owned and operated office company.

I created this planner for you, and also for me, to be portable. I bring my planner with me everywhere. It serves as a compelling invitation to turn the noise dial down and tune inward. The Fall in Love With Your Life Seasonal Planner is a trusted personal space to record your daily actions, intentions, desires and all that makes your life a unique journey worth loving. I wanted to create a system that would bring forward everything I've learned from my background in coaching, writing, goal-setting, living from the inside out – and of course, also my love of stationary.

About your Planner

This 3-month intuitive, feminine-oriented planner uses realistic and manageable micro-steps to gradually move you from where you are to where you want to be. Just like the moon comes full circle by moving gradually from one phase to another, this planner will help move you forward toward a life you love.

As you'll see, this planner even looks different, with its feminine curves that sync with the cycles of nature: the seasons, moon cycles and our own energetic cycles. It will help you establish meaningful rituals that keep you on track to loving the life you're in – no matter how life fluctuates.

It all starts with honouring your **Inner Connection**. We know that just ticking off boxes on "to-do" lists might help us feel organized, but it doesn't make us happy. The Fall in Love with Your Life Seasonal Planner aligns your daily actions to move you forward, step-by-step, to a life in complete alignment with who you are and how you most want to feel.

How this planner works

*C*reate a life you love —one week at a time with a system that makes sure your daily life is filled with activities you love and actions that move you forward toward your goals.

We start with a Vision Board, to get clear about your general aims, values and aspirations. Without knowing how, just yet, what are some qualities, circumstances, and ideas that would add up to a life you totally loved?

Next we'll tune into the seasons, aligning with the rhythms of nature to create a re-set and plan for the coming months. Using the Balance Wheel, you'll assess five areas of your life, on a scale of one to ten. As you fill in the panels, you'll begin to see which areas you feel good about or which areas you're focused on right now. From that information, you'll write some action steps — What would need to happen to move any of those areas closer to your ideal?

Next comes the actual planning part. Breaking down those juicy goals into manageable, measurable micro-steps.

First, using the Monthly Snapshots, you will fill in key dates: when school starts, birthdays, application deadlines, vacations, etc.

Then, we move to the heart of the Planner.

Each week, you will set an intention. You'll get clear about how you want to FEEL this week: Unstoppable? Chill? Supportive? Balanced? It all comes down to what your inner wisdom tells you. You'll also take a peek at the weather forecast, the moon cycle, and your energy level. You'll get a read on both the inner and outer circumstances of your life.

Here, you'll write a list of things you'd like to accomplish, identifying your top three priorities. You'll ask yourself some questions that will help strengthen your Inner Connection.

And finally, each day you'll break down those to-dos into micro-steps, things you can reasonably achieve in one balanced, lovely day.

Your calender won't be filled with activities that leave you exhausted and no more closer to your ideal life than before. Little by little you will craft a life you adore.

You don't have to do it alone

If you'd like more resources and accountability, visit emilymadill.com to learn about my Weekly Planning Sessions to keep you moving forward.

Working with Wheels

This planner is intended to help you establish an ongoing practice to step-by-step, day-by-day, reclaim a deep sense of self-worth and trust in your inner wisdom. Like the moon who is always whole, though parts of her may not be visible to our eye in the night sky – so are you. Everything you need, you already are. All parts of you belong with you. None of us is broken. Sometimes it's simply a matter of remembering who we are and reconnecting to our true nature and wholeness – no matter what storms we've weathered in life.

Working with wheels and circles

When you think of the earth, the sun, the moon, and even the clock face representing 24 hours in a day – it's easy to bring to mind a round or circular shape. The soft edge and curve of a circle also has a feminine essence. Our feminine nature is an incredible force and valuable source of wisdom. Symbolically, a circle represents wholeness and cyclical movement. When we move with our cyclical nature and soften in to who we are, it becomes much easier to see and experience life as the gift that it is.

Circular diagrams and wheels are classic tools I use in my coaching practice. A circular shape reminds us that:

- Your center is your grounding place and a rich source of wisdom.

- You are whole just as you are.

- Everything in life is cyclical — including time.

- You don't have to fit everything in one day.

- Rest and recharging is just as important as the action and doing part of your day.

- The best place to start is from where you are right now.

- All things, good and challenging, come to pass – that is the nature of life.

Working with visualization

Back in 2003, I found myself newly divorced and embarking on a different path than I had planned. Despite being in a new healthy relationship, a job I loved, and a decision to complete my university degree online, I felt afraid. What if the new relationship didn't work? What if I didn't stay motivated to finish the online courses? What if I couldn't manage the moving pieces of a successful life? While it all seems silly now, at the time my fear of failure felt larger than life. Thankfully my determination to not give up was louder than my fear.

Without realizing it, I embarked on a daily visualization practice that set me up for success. Every day before work, I laced up my shoes and headed out into the dark, rainy morning to clear my mind and rid myself of the lingering fear that clung to me. While I was running, I visualized myself at my graduation ceremony receiving my degree. I imagined my guy there cheering me on. I imagined what I was wearing and how I would smile proudly as I walked across the stage.

On my route, I ran through a neighbourhood I loved. I imagined we would one day live there and have a family and how amazing that all would feel.

I visualized not only graduating, but giving the valedictorian speech at the graduation ceremony. It all felt so real.

I would finish my run feeling alive and motivated to keep studying and showing up in my life one step, and one day at a time.

That next year I finished my degree. To my surprise, I was invited to give the valedictorian speech. I married my guy and today, we live in the neighborhood I had visualized all those rainy mornings.

It validated my belief in the power of using the mind to focus on what we *do* want to create in our life. We can either use our mind to create more detail about why life is hard, why we are afraid or why things don't work out for us. Or we can use our mind to create more detail about what we *do* want, why we want it and how it will feel, taste and look to bring our dream to life.

Let this be a fun exercise, one where you can be childlike. Don't worry about the details of "how" you are going to get from here to there. Simply focus on the "there" for the purpose of the visualization exercise.

Create your vision

My Vision

Having a vision or mind map that points in the general direction we most want to go is the first step to getting there.

For anyone unfamiliar with vision boards, it is basically a visual map of your goals utilizing your creativity. You can make one on a large poster board or in a journal. You can create one for your upcoming season on page 29.

Get clear, then get creative

Write down your goals and words that inspire you toward the life you envision right inside the circle. Add colour, doodles and make it as creative as you desire. Putting pen to paper and engaging our creative senses is a brilliant and important step towards actualizing our dreams.

Use your vision as a guide

Display your vision board where you can see it regularly (like in this planner where you will see it every day). This will help you move through that 3-week hurdle and every other obstacle that comes up.

The best part of mapping a clear vision is how it creates awareness of your deepest desires. When opportunities come up that are in line with these dreams, it becomes much easier to recognize them — and seize them.

It is an incredible feeling to begin with a thought, turn it into a goal, and one day realize you have actually achieved what you once only thought about. As you embark on yet a new season, carve out some creative time to craft a vision that is personally meaningful, realistic and in line with your goals for the year ahead.

Find your Vision Circle on page 29.

How to use the Life Balance Wheel

The balance wheel exercise is a classic tool I use in my coaching practice to help clients get a clear snapshot of their level of satisfaction in different areas of their life. This exercise also opens the door to create realistic and attainable action steps toward building a life you love.

The start of a new season is a natural segue into creating a reset. It's also a great time to make new action steps from where you are. We are always evolving and our desires and goals evolve too.

It's important to regularly take stock of what is going well, and get comfortable asking yourself what is most important to you. This simple act can have a profound effect on feeling like you are in a life of your making that you actually enjoy. The small steps we take forward from our own directive are usually the ones that lead us to our highest path.

This tool is not meant to be used to judge yourself or beat yourself up for where your level of satisfaction currently is in your life. There is no right or wrong way to live your life and it will look different for each person. The overall picture will also change throughout the week/month/year.

Step 1: Put today's date on your wheel and circle the season you are creating your wheel in. This wheel is pre-labeled with general life areas. Feel free to re-name them if you like.

Step 2: On a scale of 1 – 10 (1 low, 10 high) measure your level of satisfaction you currently have in the different areas of your life. Don't overthink, trust the first number or spot on the wheel that comes to you. This is an exercise to strengthen your intuition and self-awareness. After you have given each area a number value, shade the area in from center outward to correspond with your level of satisfaction. You can make this creative and add colors if that appeals to you.

Step 3: Now, take some time to look at the overall picture you have created. What comes to mind when you look at your life balance? What is working well? What might you like to adjust? How does it all fit together? If you have some ideas about what you might want to adjust, jot them down or come back to them when you are making your action steps.

How to create action steps

Guide for creating personalized action steps around your Seasonal Balance Wheel:

Use your completed Seasonal Balance Wheel as a reference point for making your action step(s). Note: you can add more than one action step if that seems like a right fit for you – just remember to make your steps attainable and realistic so you set yourself up to win.

Step 1: Looking at your completed Wheel, what do you notice about the big picture of the information you have created for yourself. What is standing out as important? If you were to select one area to 'up-level' your satisfaction in, which area would it be?

 * Hint: It won't always be the area with the lowest level of satisfaction. It could be an area that stands out as important right now, perhaps an area that might create more ripple effects in all of the other areas. Trust your intuition here, no need to overthink.

Step 2: After you've decided which area from your wheel you want to create an action plan for, you will use this scale to measure your level of satisfaction NOW. Circle the number representing your satisfaction now (and put the date beside it). Then you are going to circle your desired level of satisfaction you would like to up-level to in the FUTURE. Then you will put the future date beside this number indicating when you would like to reach this desired goal. Your action steps will help you get from your Now to your Desired Future.

0   1   2   3   4   5   6   7   8   9   1 0

Circle the number of the level of satisfaction in your chosen area now,
and another for your *desired* level of satisfaction in a future time of your choosing.

Step 3: Create a list of the qualities that would be present if you increased your level of satisfaction, i.e. what does a #____ of satisfaction look like for you? What will show you or tell you that you are at a #____? What would you be doing differently in your day and overall life if you had #____ level of satisfaction in this area of your life? Who else would be affected by you increasing your level of satisfaction? What is the overall value this increase would bring to your life?

Step 4: Write 3 realistic action steps you will make, over the time frame you have stated, to help you up-level your satisfaction to your desired outcome. Make these action steps personalized to you, make sure they are realistic so you'll reach your goal.

Step 5: Write how you will hold yourself accountable to your action steps. What might get in the way? How are you going to handle potential obstacles? What support can you put in place that will help you overcome anything that might get in the way of your action steps?

Step 6: How committed are you towards creating this desired level of satisfaction in your life? If you feel like you need to be more committed, what might help you feel more committed? Imagine how you would like to feel in the future and how implementing these action steps will bring value to your overall life.

When you feel ready and committed to move forward and start implementing your action steps, give yourself a huge pat on the back and a giant hug. Enjoy incorporating these steps that are a gift to you, from you.

"Investing in our well-being helps us to become well beings."
~ Emily

Find your Seasonal Balance Wheel on page 30.

Sample Seasonal Balance Wheel

WINTER | SPRING | SUMMER | AUTUMN | DATE _____

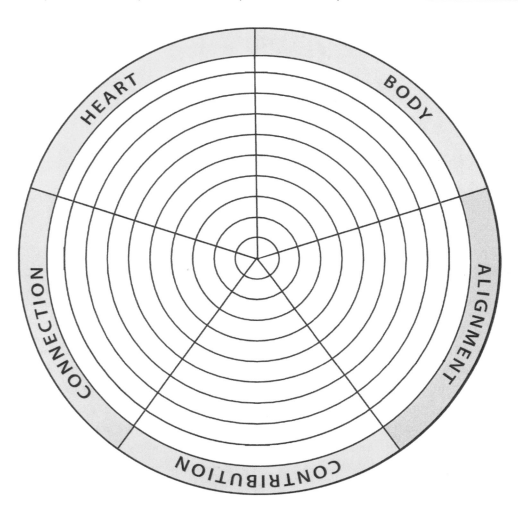

What area am I choosing to up-level? _____

Circle current satisfaction and desired up-level 0   1   2   3   4   5   6   7   8   9   10

Qualities of that up-leveled area _____

Realistic steps I will make _____

_____ By when? _____

How I plan to hold myself accountable: _____

Working with the moon's cycles

When was the last time you sat under the moon's soothing glow? Do you ever notice the moonlight and its changing shape and size as we cycle through the month? Paying attention to the moon cycle is not something new or hokey. Lunar planting is a longtime Farmer's Almanac tradition.

The moon affects the ocean tides and while there is no hard science on whether or not the moon affects human behavior – good, bad or otherwise – I do believe when we are more in tune with our natural surroundings, we invite more ease and peace into our lives. Spending time outdoors has its own meditative quality that can help us recharge.

My childhood was spent primarily outdoors in nature with other children from our neighborhood. We explored, rode bikes, built forts, learned about plants (which ones we could eat and which ones we shouldn't). We roamed free and spent all day in the fresh air. Being outside was the norm. Having to go inside meant you were sick or in trouble. I believe our bodies were in tune because of the fresh air and constant connection with nature's changing landscape. Today paints a different story for children.

Sure, kids still play outside (mine do) but there are stricter rules and parameters and distractions (often technology) that equal more screen time and less time connecting in nature. This holds true for adults, too.

In today's fast paced lifestyle, sometimes we need gentle reminders to see how wound up we have become. We must remember how important it is to get back to basics and experience pure,

uncontrived ease. Our natural environments and inner wisdom contain everything we need to get on track. We simply must start to notice, hear and be open to experiencing nature's brilliant offering each day.

When we are in sync with ourselves and our natural environment, we are more apt to make choices that consider our well-being and the well-being of humanity. When we move with life's rhythms, we are less likely to push ourselves to the point of overwhelm. The moon is the perfect daily source of inspiration to begin noticing the cyclical nature of life and how interconnected we all are.

Tracking the lunar cycle and creating rituals around the moon can be a fun and powerful way to get more in tune with nature and your own ebbs and flows. I've found tracking the moon has helped me move from experiencing life in a linear fashion to a more cyclical way. I've had a moon journal where I write down an entry, on the new and full moon, since 2015. I don't go into great detail but the practice has helped me tune into nature and my own wisdom.

Living life in a linear way is kind of like saying life is black or white – there is a striving "Type A" quality about it that doesn't allow for much variability. Whereas, living life in a more cyclical way makes room for unpredictability and fluidity to move with life – to be okay with what is before you.

There are different traditions and rituals we can create for ourselves on the new moon and full moon. These practices can help us become more aware of the cyclical nature of life. New moon and full moon rituals can become quite complex and involved, or you can follow a much simpler model like I've been doing.

On the new moon, I create a bit of space for myself in the evening and listen to some quiet calm music. I write down my intentions for the coming month, mostly how I want to feel and how I want to show up in the world. The new moon is the time for setting new intentions and hopes for your life (much like the farmers planting their seeds).

The full moon is a powerful time for letting go of what isn't serving you, or letting go of a part of yourself (habit or otherwise) that you've outgrown. I like to think of it as weeding, or clearing clutter in order to experience more ease of mind and spirit.

Usually on a full moon, I try to get outside to be under the moon's glow. Then I write in my moon journal what I'm ready to let go of in my life. Before I go to sleep, I think about those one or two things I'm ready and willing to release from my life or from my way of being. I set a silent intention around that and then I drift off to sleep.

There isn't a right or wrong way to tune into your surroundings – it's yours by design. The same goes for how we choose to set intentions, let things go, and how we decide to guide our lives – that too is a personal journey. Whether or not you decide to create a ritual for yourself around the moon, I invite you to see where there is room to connect with your natural environment. See what changes you experience with less screen time and more fresh air and green time.

How to use the Monthly Snapshots

There are 3 monthly templates for you to date and fill in to take a quick snapshot of the month.

Circle the month from the top menu, and then in the small grey box in each daily square, number the calendar. This way, the calendars can be used no matter what year or season you start this planner.

The monthly calendar is also a way to add in your important dates, holidays, appointments, etc.,

ahead of time. I like to be able to look at the season ahead in this way, so I hope it's useful to you as well.

I've also included a small space to jot down your monthly new moon intention and full moon release – if that speaks to you. *Refer to the article on page 14 to learn more about the power of paying attention to the moon. There is also a place to add your top priorities for the month relating to anything that's important to you.

Sample Monthly Snapshot

JAN | FEB | MAR | APR | MAY | JUN | JUL | AUG | SEP | OCT | NOV | DEC

♥ TOP PRIORITIES   ● NEW MOON   ◐ FULL MOON

_____   _____   _____
_____   _____   _____
_____   _____   _____
_____   _____   _____

SUN	MON	TUES	WED	THURS	FRI	SAT

Find 3 full-size Monthly Snapshots on pages 32-34.

Weekly Planning Ritual

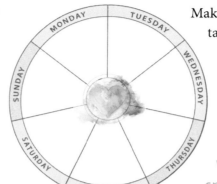

The weekly and daily planner is where you get to add the details of your life to help you stay organized, feel grounded and connected to your truth. The weekly and daily planner will also help you notice your own cyclical nature, as well as the cyclical nature of life – including the hours in a day.

Pick a day to map out your upcoming week. Choose a day you'll be able to stick to, no matter what you have going on around you. Include your responsibilities, work hours, exercise time, time with loved ones, time to yourself, appointments etc. Create a framework, so you know what you realistically have time for and how you can shape your week to feel your best.

Sunday is my ideal day to map out the upcoming week. Every Sunday, I carve out 10-15 minutes to do my weekly planning ritual.

Visit emilymadill.com to learn how you can join me for my live Weekly Planning Sessions.

Start with the Weekly Snapshot

Add your top priorities. Notice how full or spacious the week looks. This will help you avoid the trap of saying yes to too many commitments or requests for time from others. Add in your to-do's, personal, business and family-related.

Make note of how you're going to take care of yourself and recharge your batteries. This is not a part you want to skip. Taking care of ourselves is how we renew our energy, so we can actually enjoy the journey we are in.

Weekly Snapshot gives you space for:

Weekly Intention/Power Word:

Here, write your weekly intention/power word for what you want to focus on this week. What is most important to you and why? What do you want to attract into your life this week? Having one over-arching focus helps clear the mind-clutter and helps us move past obstacles during the week.

Powerful questions to help you fall in love with your life *this* week.

Heart: How do I want to feel? Sometimes we focus on what we don't want, or how we don't want to feel. That habit doesn't actually serve us, or move us any closer to what we want. It's much more empowering to connect inward and get clear on what it is we truly want. Use that desired feeling to propel you forward when you get stuck, or to inspire your actions and reactions.

Body: How will I nurture my energy, health, and body this week? When we feel connected to

and love our bodies, that feeling ripples out into different areas of our lives. This practice is all about nurturing and honouring the human body you are in – recognizing that our hormones, energy levels, focus and stamina fluctuate throughout the day, week and month. When we make it a habit to tune in, take care of ourselves and listen to what we need, we tend to move *with* our lives and invite more ease (as opposed to feeling like we are pushing uphill to the point of burnout and overwhelm).

Alignment: How do I want to show up this week? This practice is all about strengthening the inner bond you have with yourself by tuning in and asking important questions, and then honouring yourself by following through and putting it into daily practice. It is also about who do I most want to be and how can I bring her to different conversations, actions, and spaces I will be in throughout the week. This is about taking directive from your inner wisdom and truth. It's a powerful practice.

Contribution: How will I add to my community this week? Maybe this will relate to your work contributions, or how you give to your family, or surrounding community or global community. We are all interconnected and the energy we give out, does make a difference. When we put some heart and intention into that energy, it adds to the world in a positive way. We need more people adding joy and love to the equation. I love asking myself the question: What would love do here? It serves as a powerful wake up call, no matter the moment.

Connection: How will I nurture relationships this week? This could be related to relationships with the people in your household or family, maybe it's in your friendships or with coworkers, or perhaps it's with the important relationship you have with yourself. Ask the question, and trust the answer that comes. You are your own wise guide.

Moon: What is going on with the moon phase or nature? There is a little diagram you can refer to, as a way of noticing the moon's phase throughout the month. If you don't know, Google "phase of the moon." You could also add what season it is, or what's going on in your part of the world that directly relates to your natural environment.

Actions: To-do's, tasks, appointments and everything that's important to get out of your head and onto paper. Then you will prioritize 3 of your tasks as a way to ensure you don't add too many things to your week, or end up scrambling and feeling like everything is top priority. You want to avoid the feeling of overwhelm. The idea here is to create a week that spreads your energy out as evenly and balanced as possible. Make sure you have ample time for a good night's rest and that it's not all work and no play. Add your favorite activities to your list, too.

Self-Care: Ways you make time for you. This can include whatever self-care looks like to you. Maybe it will be going for a walk, or a conversation with a friend, or going to bed at a certain time, unplugging to enjoy quiet, tuning inwards or getting outdoors. Make your list personal and add lots of things, so you start to increase your awareness and gratitude for all of the things you do on a regular basis to take care of yourself.

Create an intention

Intentions are powerful statements or even a single word that encapsulates the feeling you want to experience. Your word, and intention behind the word, serves as a reminder to "be" what it is you desire.

For example, my intention and word might be calm. When I find myself overwhelmed throughout the week, I will use my intention to ask myself: how can I be calm in this moment? Then instead of beating myself up or feeling powerless, I empower myself through calming techniques. They might include things like: deep breathing, walking away from a heated discussion. It might mean holding a calm space for someone, instead of being reactive or judgmental.

If my intention is to experience connection, I can bring up this word and feeling to fuel my interactions with others. I can write a thoughtful email, compliment someone in line at the store, or carve out an hour to really listen to a loved one.

My shift in perspective isn't merely from my weekly intention-setting ritual. I shift and show up differently because all throughout the week I'm checking in with myself and adjusting my thoughts and actions based on my "connection intention."

Step 1: Set your intention for how you want to feel over the course of the next week. Get to the core of how it is you truly want to feel. What do you want the essence of your experience to be this week? Why is that important to you right now?

Step 2: Once you've nailed the part about how you want to feel, pick a word or phrase that's personally meaningful to you. Make sure it's emotionally charged and one that matches the core feeling you desire.

There isn't a right or wrong way to set your intention. It's a gift you create, to be used in a way that works best in your life. How you give and follow your directive is yours by design. The point is to use your intention as a resource that will help you feel empowered and in charge of your own happiness.

Each week there is a space in the Weekly Snapshot to add your intention. There is also space in the daily section to add that intention. I find writing out my intention each day has a way of helping it sink in a bit deeper.

Notes

_____

_____

_____

_____

_____

_____

_____

_____

_____

_____

_____

_____

Find a sample Weekly Snapshot on the following two pages.

A set of 14 week's worth of Weekly Snapshots and Daily Planners
begins on pages 36.

Sample Weekly Snapshot

WEEK OF: _____

WEEKLY INTENTION/ POWER WORD:

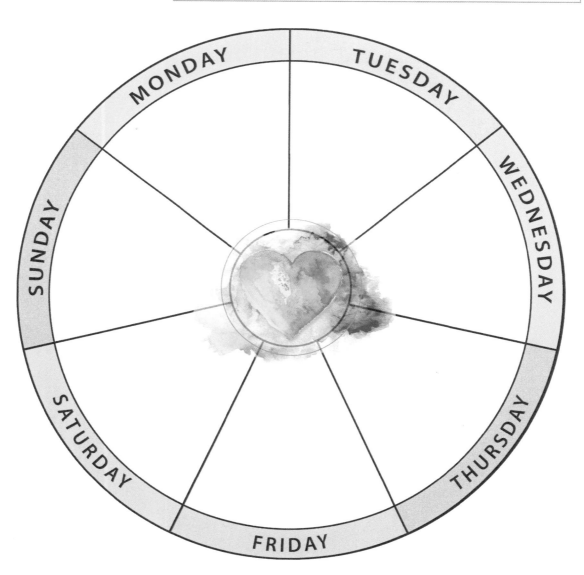

Weekly Snapshot

How will you Fall in Love With Your Life *this* week?

Heart: **How do I want to feel?**

Body: **How will I nurture my energy, health?**

Alignment: **How do I want to show up?**

Contribution: **What will I give?**

Connection: **With whom? How?**

Moon: **What cycle is the moon in?**

Waxing Moon | Full Moon | Waning Moon | New Moon

SELF-CARE

○ _____

○ _____

○ _____

TOP 3 PRIORITIES

○ 1: _____

○ 2: _____

○ 3: _____

ACTION STEPS

○ _____

○ _____

○ _____

○ _____

○ _____

○ _____

○ _____

○ _____

○ _____

○ _____

○ _____

Working with the Daily Planners

The daily planner diagram follows a circle, or 24-hour clock because I absolutely LOVE viewing the day like this. Again, this follows the feminine circle model of viewing our life, energy and time as cyclical.

Viewing our daily snapshot in this way is also a powerful reminder to add in sleep and time to recharge. I'm a huge advocate for getting regular, uninterrupted sleep. Especially now that I've experienced how much better I feel when I'm well-rested. I keep my phone out of my bedroom on purpose to avoid the temptation of distraction our technology and phones tend to create. Instead, I use an old-fashioned alarm clock.

When I sit down to do my weekly planning ritual, I pre-fill out some of the items on the daily planner ahead of time. I write my daily to-do's or appointments etc. right next to the time within the circle. Then each morning I open my planner to that day and add any extra items or reminders.

Gratitude

I jot down the first thing that comes to mind that I'm grateful for. Having a daily gratitude practice is an easy and powerful thing to do –especially when we do it regularly. What we focus on, tends to grow in our awareness and perception. Having a daily gratitude practice is a part of those small steps toward noticing and feeling like you are in a life you love.

Inner wisdom

I left a space for Inner Guidance. Take a moment at the beginning of each day to tune in to your own Inner Wisdom. You can also add any inner wisdom or reflections that come up during the day. This is a great invitation to tune inward and to start to notice the themes and inner nudges that you might otherwise miss in this noisy, busy world. You may also start to notice repetitive words or core values that surface.

"Don't delay your happiness for later, jump in and love the life you are in!"
~ Emily

Sample Daily Planner

SUN | MON | TUES | WED | THURS | FRI | SAT   DATE _____

TODAY I AM GRATEFUL FOR: _____

INNER GUIDANCE: _____

REMINDERS/NOTES: _____

Waxing Moon   Full Moon   Waning Moon   New Moon

12pm
11am
1pm
10am
2pm
9am
3pm
8am
4pm
7am
5pm
6am
6pm
5am
7pm
4am
8pm
3am
9pm
2am
10pm
1am
12am
11pm

Fall in Love with Your Life

3-MONTH
SEASONAL PLANNER

Start date: _____

Season: _____

My Vision

Seasonal Balance Wheel

WINTER | SPRING | SUMMER | AUTUMN | DATE _____

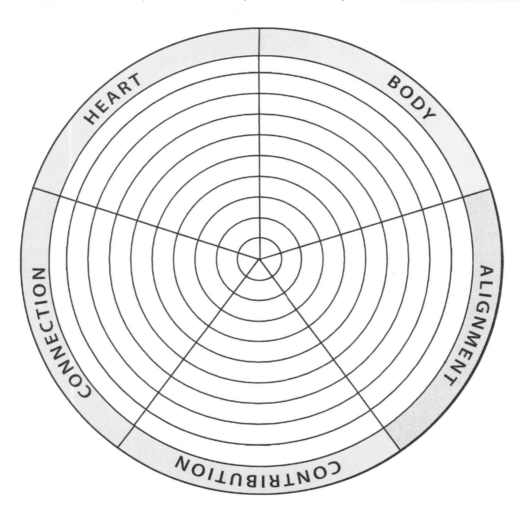

What area am I choosing to up-level? _____

Circle current satisfaction and desired up-level   0   1   2   3   4   5   6   7   8   9   10

Qualities of that up-leveled area _____

Realistic steps I will make _____

_____ By when? _____

How I plan to hold myself accountable: _____

Notes

_____

_____

_____

_____

_____

_____

_____

_____

_____

_____

_____

_____

_____

_____

_____

_____

To order your next Fall in Love With Your Life Seasonal Planner visit: emilymadill.com

Monthly Snapshot

JAN | FEB | MAR | APR | MAY | JUN | JUL | AUG | SEP | OCT | NOV | DEC

TOP PRIORITIES   NEW MOON   FULL MOON

SUN	MON	TUES	WED	THURS	FRI	SAT

Monthly Snapshot

JAN | FEB | MAR | APR | MAY | JUN | JUL | AUG | SEP | OCT | NOV | DEC

TOP PRIORITIES

NEW MOON

FULL MOON

SUN	MON	TUES	WED	THURS	FRI	SAT

Monthly Snapshot

JAN | FEB | MAR | APR | MAY | JUN | JUL | AUG | SEP | OCT | NOV | DEC

TOP PRIORITIES

NEW MOON

FULL MOON

SUN	MON	TUES	WED	THURS	FRI	SAT

Notes

_____

_____

_____

_____

_____

January 2021						
S	M	T	W	Th	F	S
					1	2
3	4	5	6	7	8	9
10	11	12	13	14	15	16
17	18	19	20	21	22	23
24	25	26	27	28	29	30
31						

February 2021						
S	M	T	W	Th	F	S
	1	2	3	4	5	6
7	8	9	10	11	12	13
14	15	16	17	18	19	20
21	22	23	24	25	26	27
28						

March 2021						
S	M	T	W	Th	F	S
	1	2	3	4	5	6
7	8	9	10	11	12	13
14	15	16	17	18	19	20
21	22	23	24	25	26	27
28	29	30	31			

April 2021						
S	M	T	W	Th	F	S
				1	2	3
4	5	6	7	8	9	10
11	12	13	14	15	16	17
18	19	20	21	22	23	24
25	26	27	28	29	30	

May 2021						
S	M	T	W	Th	F	S
						1
2	3	4	5	6	7	8
9	10	11	12	13	14	15
16	17	18	19	20	21	22
23	24	25	26	27	28	29
30	31					

June 2021						
S	M	T	W	Th	F	S
		1	2	3	4	5
6	7	8	9	10	11	12
13	14	15	16	17	18	19
20	21	22	23	24	25	26
27	28	29	30			

July 2021						
S	M	T	W	Th	F	S
				1	2	3
4	5	6	7	8	9	10
11	12	13	14	15	16	17
18	19	20	21	22	23	24
25	26	27	28	29	30	31

August 2021						
S	M	T	W	Th	F	S
1	2	3	4	5	6	7
8	9	10	11	12	13	14
15	16	17	18	19	20	21
22	23	24	25	26	27	28
29	30	31				

September 2021						
S	M	T	W	Th	F	S
		1	2	3	4	
5	6	7	8	9	10	11
12	13	14	15	16	17	18
19	20	21	22	23	24	25
26	27	28	29	30		

October 2021						
S	M	T	W	Th	F	S
					1	2
3	4	5	6	7	8	9
10	11	12	13	14	15	16
17	18	19	20	21	22	23
24	25	26	27	28	29	30
31						

November 2021						
S	M	T	W	Th	F	S
	1	2	3	4	5	6
7	8	9	10	11	12	13
14	15	16	17	18	19	20
21	22	23	24	25	26	27
28	29	30				

December 2021						
S	M	T	W	Th	F	S
			1	2	3	4
5	6	7	8	9	10	11
12	13	14	15	16	17	18
19	20	21	22	23	24	25
26	27	28	29	30	31	

To order your next Fall in Love With Your Life Seasonal Planner visit: emilymadill.com

Weekly Snapshot

WEEK OF: _____

WEEKLY INTENTION/
POWER WORD:

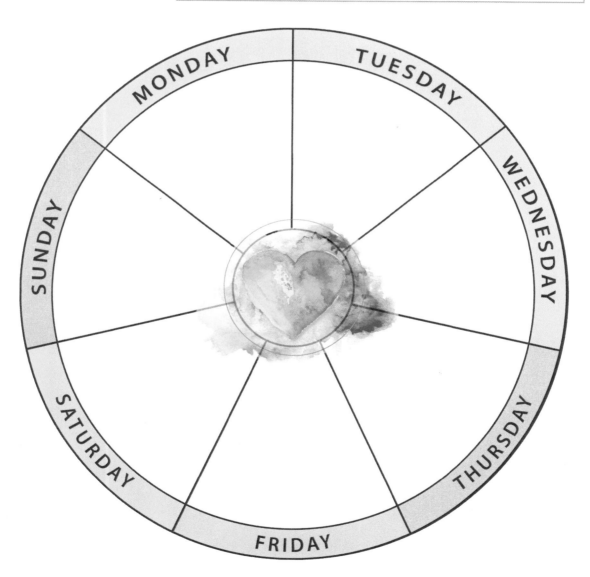

MONDAY

TUESDAY

WEDNESDAY

THURSDAY

FRIDAY

SATURDAY

SUNDAY

Weekly Snapshot

How will you Fall in Love With Your Life *this* week?

Heart: How do I want to feel?

Body: How will I nurture my energy, health?

Alignment: How do I want to show up?

Contribution: What will I give?

Connection: With whom? How?

Moon: What cycle is the moon in?

Waxing Moon   Full Moon   Waning Moon   New Moon

SELF-CARE

O _____

O _____

O _____

TOP 3 PRIORITIES

O 1: _____

O 2: _____

O 3: _____

ACTION STEPS

O _____

O _____

O _____

O _____

O _____

O _____

O _____

O _____

O _____

O _____

O _____

Daily Planner

SUN | MON | TUES | WED | THURS | FRI | SAT   DATE _____

TODAY I AM GRATEFUL FOR: _____

INNER GUIDANCE: _____

REMINDERS/NOTES: _____

Waxing Moon   Full Moon   Waning Moon   New Moon

12pm
11am   1pm
10am   2pm
9am   3pm
8am   4pm
7am   5pm
6am   6pm
5am   7pm
4am   8pm
3am   9pm
2am   10pm
1am   12am   11pm

Daily Planner

SUN | MON | TUES | WED | THURS | FRI | SAT   DATE _____

TODAY I AM GRATEFUL FOR: _____

INNER GUIDANCE: _____

REMINDERS/NOTES: _____

Waxing Moon   Full Moon   Waning Moon   New Moon

12pm
11am   1pm
10am   2pm
9am   3pm
8am   4pm
7am   5pm
6am   6pm
5am   7pm
4am   8pm
3am   9pm
2am   10pm
1am   12am   11pm

Daily Planner

TODAY I AM GRATEFUL FOR: _____

INNER GUIDANCE: _____

REMINDERS/NOTES: _____

Waxing Moon   Full Moon   Waning Moon   New Moon

12pm
11am
1pm
10am
2pm
9am
3pm
8am
4pm
7am
5pm
6am
6pm
5am
7pm
4am
8pm
3am
9pm
2am
10pm
1am
12am
11pm

Daily Planner

SUN | MON | TUES | WED | THURS | FRI | SAT   DATE _____

TODAY I AM GRATEFUL FOR: _____

INNER GUIDANCE: _____

REMINDERS/NOTES: _____

| Waxing Moon | Full Moon | Waning Moon | New Moon |

12pm
11am
1pm
10am
2pm
9am
3pm
8am
4pm
7am
5pm
6am
6pm
5am
7pm
4am
8pm
3am
9pm
2am
10pm
1am
12am
11pm

Daily Planner

SUN | MON | TUES | WED | THURS | FRI | SAT   DATE _____

TODAY I AM GRATEFUL FOR: _____

INNER GUIDANCE: _____

REMINDERS/NOTES: _____

Waxing Moon   Full Moon   Waning Moon   New Moon

12pm
11am   1pm
10am   2pm
9am   3pm
8am   4pm
7am   5pm
6am   6pm
5am   7pm
4am   8pm
3am   9pm
2am   10pm
1am   12am   11pm

Daily Planner

SUN | MON | TUES | WED | THURS | FRI | SAT   DATE _____

TODAY I AM GRATEFUL FOR: _____

INNER GUIDANCE: _____

REMINDERS/NOTES: _____

Waxing Moon   Full Moon   Waning Moon   New Moon

12pm
1pm
11am
2pm
10am
3pm
9am
4pm
8am
5pm
7am
6pm
6am
7pm
5am
8pm
4am
9pm
3am
10pm
2am
11pm
1am   12am

Daily Planner

SUN | MON | TUES | WED | THURS | FRI | SAT   DATE _____

TODAY I AM GRATEFUL FOR: _____

INNER GUIDANCE: _____

REMINDERS/NOTES: _____

Waxing Moon   Full Moon   Waning Moon   New Moon

12pm
11am   1pm
10am   2pm
9am   3pm
8am   4pm
7am   5pm
6am   6pm
5am   7pm
4am   8pm
3am   9pm
2am   10pm
1am   12am   11pm

Notes

_____

_____

_____

_____

_____

_____

_____

_____

_____

_____

_____

_____

_____

_____

_____

_____

To order your next Fall in Love With Your Life Seasonal Planner visit: emilymadill.com

Weekly Snapshot

WEEK OF: _____

WEEKLY INTENTION/
POWER WORD:

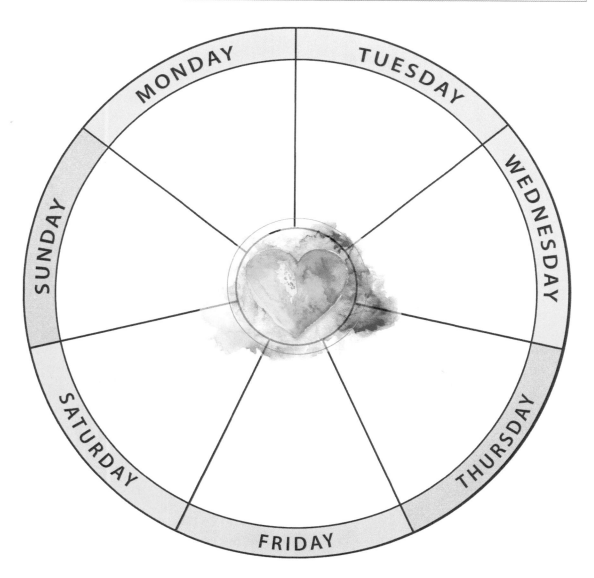

MONDAY

TUESDAY

WEDNESDAY

THURSDAY

FRIDAY

SATURDAY

SUNDAY

Weekly Snapshot

How will you Fall in Love With Your Life *this* week?

Heart: **How do I want to feel?**

Body: **How will I nurture my energy, health?**

Alignment: **How do I want to show up?**

Contribution: **What will I give?**

Connection: **With whom? How?**

Moon: **What cycle is the moon in?**

| Waxing Moon | Full Moon | Waning Moon | New Moon |

SELF-CARE

○ _____

○ _____

○ _____

TOP 3 PRIORITIES

○ 1: _____

○ 2: _____

○ 3: _____

ACTION STEPS

○ _____

○ _____

○ _____

○ _____

○ _____

○ _____

○ _____

○ _____

○ _____

○ _____

Daily Planner

TODAY I AM GRATEFUL FOR: _____

INNER GUIDANCE: _____

REMINDERS/NOTES: _____

Waxing Moon   Full Moon   Waning Moon   New Moon

12pm
11am   1pm
10am   2pm
9am   3pm
8am   4pm
7am   5pm
6am   6pm
5am   7pm
4am   8pm
3am   9pm
2am   10pm
1am   12am   11pm

Daily Planner

SUN | MON | TUES | WED | THURS | FRI | SAT   DATE _____

TODAY I AM GRATEFUL FOR: _____

INNER GUIDANCE: _____

REMINDERS/NOTES: _____

Waxing
Moon

Full
Moon

Waning
Moon

New
Moon

12pm
11am
1pm
10am
2pm
9am
3pm
8am
4pm
7am
5pm
6am
6pm
5am
7pm
4am
8pm
3am
9pm
2am
10pm
1am
11pm
12am

Daily Planner

SUN | MON | TUES | WED | THURS | FRI | SAT   DATE _____

TODAY I AM GRATEFUL FOR: _____

INNER GUIDANCE: _____

REMINDERS/NOTES: _____

Waxing Moon   Full Moon   Waning Moon   New Moon

12pm
11am   1pm
10am   2pm
9am   3pm
8am   4pm
7am   5pm
6am   6pm
5am   7pm
4am   8pm
3am   9pm
2am   10pm
1am   12am   11pm

Daily Planner

TODAY I AM GRATEFUL FOR: _____

INNER GUIDANCE: _____

REMINDERS/NOTES: _____

Waxing Moon   Full Moon   Waning Moon   New Moon

12pm
11am   1pm
10am   2pm
9am   3pm
8am   4pm
7am   5pm
6am   6pm
5am   7pm
4am   8pm
3am   9pm
2am   10pm
1am   12am   11pm

Daily Planner

SUN | MON | TUES | WED | THURS | FRI | SAT   DATE _____

TODAY I AM GRATEFUL FOR: _____

INNER GUIDANCE: _____

REMINDERS/NOTES: _____

Waxing Moon   Full Moon   Waning Moon   New Moon

12pm
11am
1pm
10am
2pm
9am
3pm
8am
4pm
7am
5pm
6am
6pm
5am
7pm
4am
8pm
3am
9pm
2am
10pm
1am
12am
11pm

Daily Planner

SUN | MON | TUES | WED | THURS | FRI | SAT   DATE _____

TODAY I AM GRATEFUL FOR: _____

INNER GUIDANCE: _____

REMINDERS/NOTES: _____

Waxing Moon   Full Moon   Waning Moon   New Moon

12pm
11am   1pm
10am   2pm
9am   3pm
8am   4pm
7am   5pm
6am   6pm
5am   7pm
4am   8pm
3am   9pm
2am   10pm
1am   12am   11pm

Daily Planner

SUN | MON | TUES | WED | THURS | FRI | SAT   DATE _____

TODAY I AM GRATEFUL FOR: _____

INNER GUIDANCE: _____

REMINDERS/NOTES: _____

Waxing Moon   Full Moon   Waning Moon   New Moon

12pm
11am   1pm
10am   2pm
9am   3pm
8am   4pm
7am   5pm
6am   6pm
5am   7pm
4am   8pm
3am   9pm
2am   10pm
1am   12am   11pm

Notes

_____

_____

_____

_____

_____

_____

_____

_____

_____

_____

_____

_____

_____

_____

_____

To order your next Fall in Love With Your Life Seasonal Planner visit: emilymadill.com

Weekly Snapshot

WEEK OF: _____

WEEKLY INTENTION/ POWER WORD:

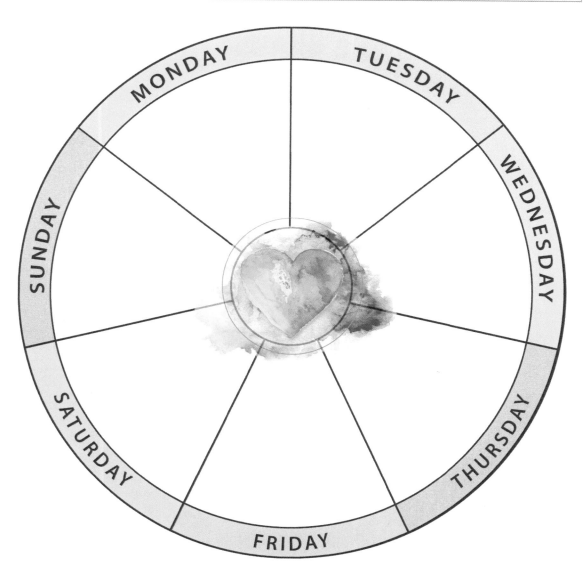

Weekly Snapshot

How will you Fall in Love With Your Life *this* week?

Heart: **How do I want to feel?**

Body: **How will I nurture my energy, health?**

Alignment: **How do I want to show up?**

Contribution: **What will I give?**

Connection: **With whom? How?**

Moon: **What cycle is the moon in?**

Waxing Moon   Full Moon   Waning Moon   New Moon

SELF-CARE

○ _____

○ _____

○ _____

TOP 3 PRIORITIES

○ 1: _____

○ 2: _____

○ 3: _____

ACTION STEPS

○ _____

○ _____

○ _____

○ _____

○ _____

○ _____

○ _____

○ _____

○ _____

○ _____

○ _____

Daily Planner

SUN | MON | TUES | WED | THURS | FRI | SAT   DATE _____

TODAY I AM GRATEFUL FOR: _____

INNER GUIDANCE: _____

REMINDERS/NOTES: _____

Waxing Moon   Full Moon   Waning Moon   New Moon

12pm
11am   1pm
10am   2pm
9am   3pm
8am   4pm
7am   5pm
6am   6pm
5am   7pm
4am   8pm
3am   9pm
2am   10pm
1am   12am   11pm

Daily Planner

SUN | MON | TUES | WED | THURS | FRI | SAT   DATE _____

TODAY I AM GRATEFUL FOR: _____

INNER GUIDANCE: _____

REMINDERS/NOTES: _____

Waxing Moon	Full Moon	Waning Moon	New Moon

11am · 12pm · 1pm
10am · · 2pm
9am · · 3pm
8am · · 4pm
7am · · 5pm
6am · · 6pm
5am · · 7pm
4am · · 8pm
3am · · 9pm
2am · · 10pm
1am · 12am · 11pm

Daily Planner

SUN | MON | TUES | WED | THURS | FRI | SAT   DATE _____

TODAY I AM GRATEFUL FOR: _____

INNER GUIDANCE: _____

REMINDERS/NOTES: _____

Waxing Moon   Full Moon   Waning Moon   New Moon

12pm
11am
1pm
10am
2pm
9am
3pm
8am
4pm
7am
5pm
6am
6pm
5am
7pm
4am
8pm
3am
9pm
2am
10pm
1am
12am
11pm

Daily Planner

SUN | MON | TUES | WED | THURS | FRI | SAT   DATE _____

TODAY I AM GRATEFUL FOR: _____

INNER GUIDANCE: _____

REMINDERS/NOTES: _____

Waxing Moon   Full Moon   Waning Moon   New Moon

12pm
11am   1pm
10am   2pm
9am   3pm
8am   4pm
7am   5pm
6am   6pm
5am   7pm
4am   8pm
3am   9pm
2am   10pm
1am   12am   11pm

Daily Planner

SUN | MON | TUES | WED | THURS | FRI | SAT   DATE _____

TODAY I AM GRATEFUL FOR: _____

INNER GUIDANCE: _____

REMINDERS/NOTES: _____

Waxing Moon   Full Moon   Waning Moon   New Moon

12pm
11am   1pm
10am   2pm
9am   3pm
8am   4pm
7am   5pm
6am   6pm
5am   7pm
4am   8pm
3am   9pm
2am   10pm
1am   12am   11pm

Daily Planner

SUN | MON | TUES | WED | THURS | FRI | SAT   DATE _____

TODAY I AM GRATEFUL FOR: _____

INNER GUIDANCE: _____

REMINDERS/NOTES: _____

Waxing Moon   Full Moon   Waning Moon   New Moon

12pm
11am
1pm
10am
2pm
9am
3pm
8am
4pm
7am
5pm
6am
6pm
5am
7pm
4am
8pm
3am
9pm
2am
10pm
1am
12am
11pm

Daily Planner

SUN | MON | TUES | WED | THURS | FRI | SAT   DATE _____

TODAY I AM GRATEFUL FOR: _____

INNER GUIDANCE: _____

REMINDERS/NOTES: _____

Waxing Moon   Full Moon   Waning Moon   New Moon

12pm
11am   1pm
10am   2pm
9am   3pm
8am   4pm
7am   5pm
6am   6pm
5am   7pm
4am   8pm
3am   9pm
2am   10pm
1am   12am   11pm

Notes

_____

_____

_____

_____

_____

_____

_____

_____

_____

_____

_____

_____

_____

_____

_____

Weekly Snapshot

WEEK OF: _____

WEEKLY INTENTION/
POWER WORD:

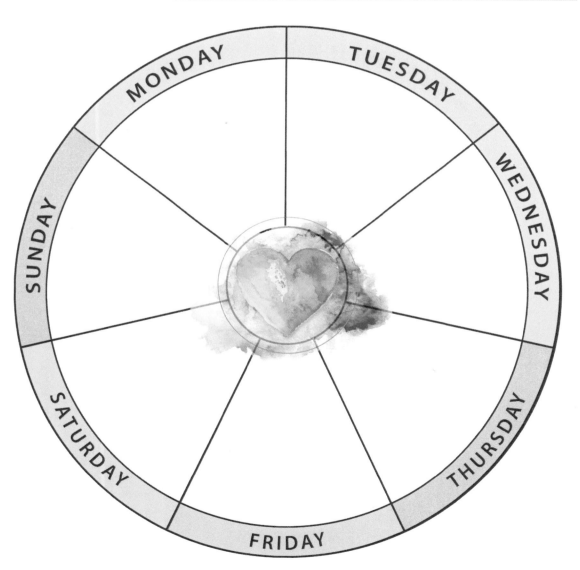

MONDAY

TUESDAY

WEDNESDAY

SUNDAY

THURSDAY

SATURDAY

FRIDAY

Weekly Snapshot

How will you Fall in Love With Your Life *this* week?

Heart: How do I want to feel?

Body: How will I nurture my energy, health?

Alignment: How do I want to show up?

Contribution: What will I give?

Connection: With whom? How?

Moon: What cycle is the moon in?

Waxing Moon   Full Moon   Waning Moon   New Moon

SELF-CARE

○ _____

○ _____

○ _____

TOP 3 PRIORITIES

○ 1: _____

○ 2: _____

○ 3: _____

ACTION STEPS

○ _____

○ _____

○ _____

○ _____

○ _____

○ _____

○ _____

○ _____

○ _____

○ _____

○ _____

Daily Planner

SUN | MON | TUES | WED | THURS | FRI | SAT   DATE _____

TODAY I AM GRATEFUL FOR: _____

INNER GUIDANCE: _____

REMINDERS/NOTES: _____

Waxing Moon   Full Moon   Waning Moon   New Moon

12pm
11am   1pm
10am   2pm
9am   3pm
8am   4pm
7am   5pm
6am   6pm
5am   7pm
4am   8pm
3am   9pm
2am   10pm
1am   12am   11pm

Daily Planner

SUN | MON | TUES | WED | THURS | FRI | SAT   DATE _____

TODAY I AM GRATEFUL FOR: _____

INNER GUIDANCE: _____

REMINDERS/NOTES: _____

Waxing Moon   Full Moon   Waning Moon   New Moon

12pm
11am   1pm
10am   2pm
9am   3pm
8am   4pm
7am   5pm
6am   6pm
5am   7pm
4am   8pm
3am   9pm
2am   10pm
1am   12am   11pm

Daily Planner

TODAY I AM GRATEFUL FOR: _____

INNER GUIDANCE: _____

REMINDERS/NOTES: _____

Waxing Moon   Full Moon   Waning Moon   New Moon

12pm
11am   1pm
10am   2pm
9am   3pm
8am   4pm
7am   5pm
6am   6pm
5am   7pm
4am   8pm
3am   9pm
2am   10pm
1am   12am   11pm

Daily Planner

SUN | MON | TUES | WED | THURS | FRI | SAT   DATE _____

TODAY I AM GRATEFUL FOR: _____

INNER GUIDANCE: _____

REMINDERS/NOTES: _____

Waxing Moon   Full Moon   Waning Moon   New Moon

12pm
11am   1pm
10am   2pm
9am   3pm
8am   4pm
7am   5pm
6am   6pm
5am   7pm
4am   8pm
3am   9pm
2am   10pm
1am   12am   11pm

Daily Planner

SUN | MON | TUES | WED | THURS | FRI | SAT   DATE _____

TODAY I AM GRATEFUL FOR: _____

INNER GUIDANCE: _____

REMINDERS/NOTES: _____

Waxing Moon   Full Moon   Waning Moon   New Moon

12pm
11am 1pm
10am 2pm
9am 3pm
8am 4pm
7am 5pm
6am 6pm
5am 7pm
4am 8pm
3am 9pm
2am 10pm
1am 12am 11pm

Daily Planner

SUN | MON | TUES | WED | THURS | FRI | SAT   DATE _____

TODAY I AM GRATEFUL FOR: _____

INNER GUIDANCE: _____

REMINDERS/NOTES: _____

Waxing Moon   Full Moon   Waning Moon   New Moon

12pm
11am   1pm
10am   2pm
9am   3pm
8am   4pm
7am   5pm
6am   6pm
5am   7pm
4am   8pm
3am   9pm
2am   10pm
1am 12am 11pm

Daily Planner

SUN | MON | TUES | WED | THURS | FRI | SAT   DATE _____

TODAY I AM GRATEFUL FOR: _____

INNER GUIDANCE: _____

REMINDERS/NOTES: _____

Waxing Moon   Full Moon   Waning Moon   New Moon

12pm
11am   1pm
10am   2pm
9am   3pm
8am   4pm
7am   5pm
6am   6pm
5am   7pm
4am   8pm
3am   9pm
2am   10pm
1am   12am   11pm

Notes

_____

_____

_____

_____

_____

_____

_____

_____

_____

_____

_____

_____

_____

_____

_____

To order your next Fall in Love With Your Life Seasonal Planner visit: emilymadill.com

Weekly Snapshot

WEEK OF: _____

WEEKLY INTENTION/ POWER WORD:

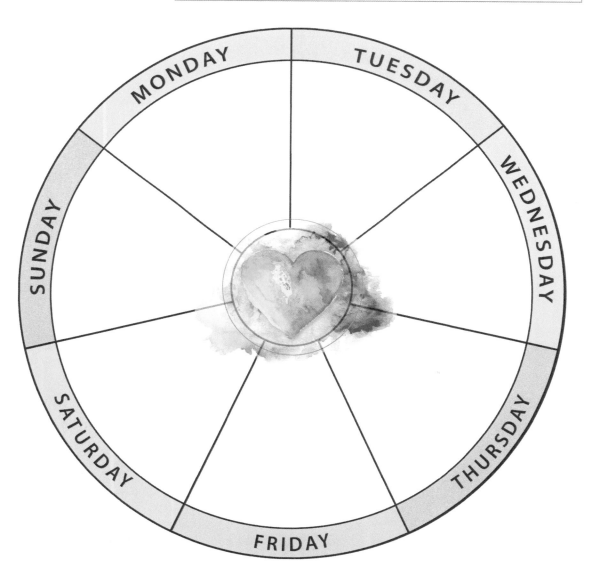

Weekly Snapshot

How will you Fall in Love With Your Life *this* week?

Heart: **How do I want to feel?**

Body: **How will I nurture my energy, health?**

Alignment: **How do I want to show up?**

Contribution: **What will I give?**

Connection: **With whom? How?**

Moon: **What cycle is the moon in?**

Waxing Moon   Full Moon   Waning Moon   New Moon

SELF-CARE

○ _____

○ _____

○ _____

TOP 3 PRIORITIES

○ 1: _____

○ 2: _____

○ 3: _____

ACTION STEPS

○ _____

○ _____

○ _____

○ _____

○ _____

○ _____

○ _____

○ _____

○ _____

○ _____

○ _____

Daily Planner

SUN | MON | TUES | WED | THURS | FRI | SAT   DATE _____

TODAY I AM GRATEFUL FOR: _____

INNER GUIDANCE: _____

REMINDERS/NOTES: _____

Waxing Moon   Full Moon   Waning Moon   New Moon

12pm
11am   1pm
10am   2pm
9am   3pm
8am   4pm
7am   5pm
6am   6pm
5am   7pm
4am   8pm
3am   9pm
2am   10pm
1am   11pm
12am

Daily Planner

SUN | MON | TUES | WED | THURS | FRI | SAT   DATE _____

TODAY I AM GRATEFUL FOR: _____

INNER GUIDANCE: _____

REMINDERS/NOTES: _____

Waxing Moon   Full Moon   Waning Moon   New Moon

12pm
11am   1pm
10am   2pm
9am   3pm
8am   4pm
7am   5pm
6am   6pm
5am   7pm
4am   8pm
3am   9pm
2am   10pm
1am   12am   11pm

Daily Planner

SUN | MON | TUES | WED | THURS | FRI | SAT   DATE _____

TODAY I AM GRATEFUL FOR: _____

INNER GUIDANCE: _____

REMINDERS/NOTES: _____

Waxing Moon   Full Moon   Waning Moon   New Moon

12pm
11am 1pm
10am 2pm
9am 3pm
8am 4pm
7am 5pm
6am 6pm
5am 7pm
4am 8pm
3am 9pm
2am 10pm
1am 12am 11pm

Daily Planner

SUN | MON | TUES | WED | THURS | FRI | SAT   DATE _____

TODAY I AM GRATEFUL FOR: _____

INNER GUIDANCE: _____

REMINDERS/NOTES: _____

Waxing Moon   Full Moon   Waning Moon   New Moon

12pm
11am   1pm
10am   2pm
9am   3pm
8am   4pm
7am   5pm
6am   6pm
5am   7pm
4am   8pm
3am   9pm
2am   10pm
1am   12am   11pm

Daily Planner

SUN | MON | TUES | WED | THURS | FRI | SAT   DATE _____

TODAY I AM GRATEFUL FOR: _____

INNER GUIDANCE: _____

REMINDERS/NOTES: _____

Waxing
Moon

Full
Moon

Waning
Moon

New
Moon

12pm
11am
10am
1pm
9am
2pm
8am
3pm
7am
4pm
6am
5pm
5am
6pm
4am
7pm
3am
8pm
2am
9pm
1am
10pm
12am
11pm

Daily Planner

SUN | MON | TUES | WED | THURS | FRI | SAT   DATE _____

TODAY I AM GRATEFUL FOR: _____

INNER GUIDANCE: _____

REMINDERS/NOTES: _____

Waxing Moon   Full Moon   Waning Moon   New Moon

12pm
11am 1pm
10am 2pm
9am 3pm
8am 4pm
7am 5pm
6am 6pm
5am 7pm
4am 8pm
3am 9pm
2am 10pm
1am 12am 11pm

Daily Planner

SUN | MON | TUES | WED | THURS | FRI | SAT   DATE _____

TODAY I AM GRATEFUL FOR: _____

INNER GUIDANCE: _____

REMINDERS/NOTES: _____

Waxing Moon   Full Moon   Waning Moon   New Moon

12pm
11am   1pm
10am   2pm
9am   3pm
8am   4pm
7am   5pm
6am   6pm
5am   7pm
4am   8pm
3am   9pm
2am   10pm
1am   12am   11pm

Notes

_____

_____

_____

_____

_____

_____

_____

_____

_____

_____

_____

_____

_____

_____

_____

Weekly Snapshot

WEEK OF: _____

WEEKLY INTENTION/ POWER WORD: [   ]

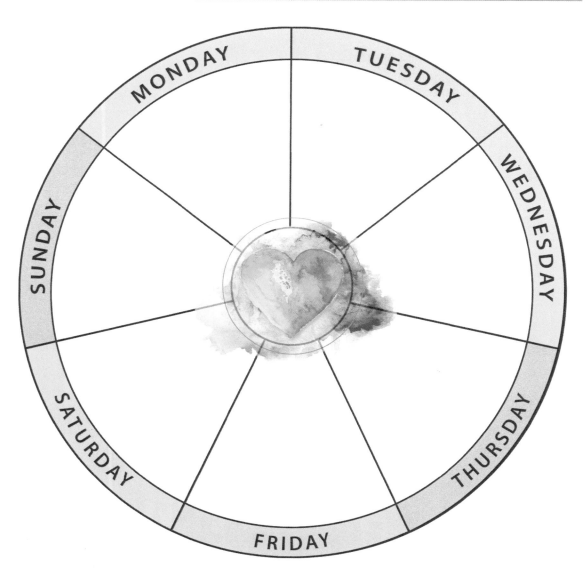

MONDAY · TUESDAY · WEDNESDAY · THURSDAY · FRIDAY · SATURDAY · SUNDAY

Weekly Snapshot

How will you Fall in Love With Your Life *this* week?

Heart: **How do I want to feel?**

Body: **How will I nurture my energy, health?**

Alignment: **How do I want to show up?**

Contribution: **What will I give?**

Connection: **With whom? How?**

Moon: **What cycle is the moon in?**

Waxing
Moon

Full
Moon

Waning
Moon

New
Moon

SELF-CARE

○ _____

○ _____

○ _____

TOP 3 PRIORITIES

○ 1: _____

○ 2: _____

○ 3: _____

ACTION STEPS

○ _____

○ _____

○ _____

○ _____

○ _____

○ _____

○ _____

○ _____

○ _____

○ _____

○ _____

Daily Planner

SUN | MON | TUES | WED | THURS | FRI | SAT   DATE _____

TODAY I AM GRATEFUL FOR: _____

INNER GUIDANCE: _____

REMINDERS/NOTES: _____

Waxing Moon   Full Moon   Waning Moon   New Moon

12pm
11am   1pm
10am   2pm
9am   3pm
8am   4pm
7am   5pm
6am   6pm
5am   7pm
4am   8pm
3am   9pm
2am   10pm
1am   12am   11pm

Daily Planner

SUN | MON | TUES | WED | THURS | FRI | SAT   DATE _____

TODAY I AM GRATEFUL FOR: _____

INNER GUIDANCE: _____

REMINDERS/NOTES: _____

Waxing Moon   Full Moon   Waning Moon   New Moon

12pm
11am
1pm
10am
2pm
9am
3pm
8am
4pm
7am
5pm
6am
6pm
5am
7pm
4am
8pm
3am
9pm
2am
10pm
1am
12am
11pm

Daily Planner

SUN | MON | TUES | WED | THURS | FRI | SAT   DATE _____

TODAY I AM GRATEFUL FOR: _____

INNER GUIDANCE: _____

REMINDERS/NOTES: _____

Waxing Moon   Full Moon   Waning Moon   New Moon

12pm
11am   1pm
10am   2pm
9am   3pm
8am   4pm
7am   5pm
6am   6pm
5am   7pm
4am   8pm
3am   9pm
2am   10pm
1am   12am   11pm

Daily Planner

SUN | MON | TUES | WED | THURS | FRI | SAT   DATE _____

TODAY I AM GRATEFUL FOR: _____

INNER GUIDANCE: _____

REMINDERS/NOTES: _____

Waxing Moon   Full Moon   Waning Moon   New Moon

12pm
11am   1pm
10am   2pm
9am   3pm
8am   4pm
7am   5pm
6am   6pm
5am   7pm
4am   8pm
3am   9pm
2am   10pm
1am   12am   11pm

Daily Planner

SUN | MON | TUES | WED | THURS | FRI | SAT   DATE _____

TODAY I AM GRATEFUL FOR: _____

INNER GUIDANCE: _____

REMINDERS/NOTES: _____

Waxing Moon   Full Moon   Waning Moon   New Moon

12pm · 11am · 1pm · 10am · 2pm · 9am · 3pm · 8am · 4pm · 7am · 5pm · 6am · 6pm · 5am · 7pm · 4am · 8pm · 3am · 9pm · 2am · 10pm · 1am · 12am · 11pm

Daily Planner

SUN | MON | TUES | WED | THURS | FRI | SAT   DATE _____

TODAY I AM GRATEFUL FOR: _____

INNER GUIDANCE: _____

REMINDERS/NOTES: _____

Waxing Moon   Full Moon   Waning Moon   New Moon

12pm
11am
10am
9am
8am
7am
6am
5am
4am
3am
2am
1am
12am
11pm
10pm
9pm
8pm
7pm
6pm
5pm
4pm
3pm
2pm
1pm

Daily Planner

SUN | MON | TUES | WED | THURS | FRI | SAT   DATE _____

TODAY I AM GRATEFUL FOR: _____

INNER GUIDANCE: _____

REMINDERS/NOTES: _____

Waxing Moon   Full Moon   Waning Moon   New Moon

12pm
11am   1pm
10am   2pm
9am   3pm
8am   4pm
7am   5pm
6am   6pm
5am   7pm
4am   8pm
3am   9pm
2am   10pm
1am   12am   11pm

Notes

_____

_____

_____

_____

_____

_____

_____

_____

_____

_____

_____

_____

_____

_____

_____

To order your next Fall in Love With Your Life Seasonal Planner visit: emilymadill.com

Weekly Snapshot

WEEK OF: _____

WEEKLY INTENTION/ POWER WORD: [_____]

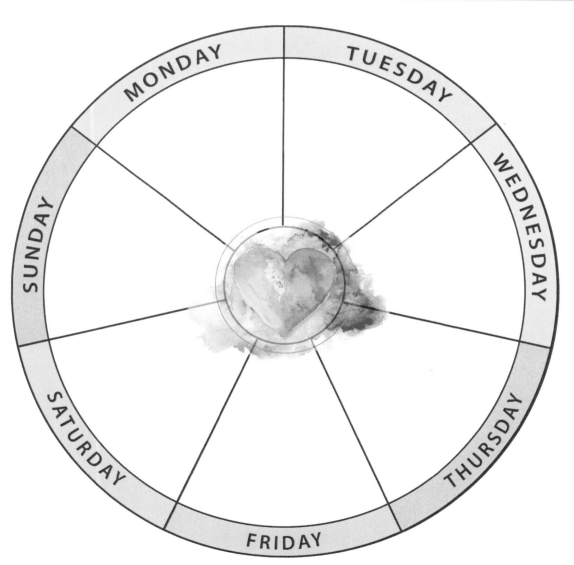

Weekly Snapshot

How will you Fall in Love With Your Life *this* week?

Heart: **How do I want to feel?**

Body: **How will I nurture my energy, health?**

Alignment: **How do I want to show up?**

Contribution: **What will I give?**

Connection: **With whom? How?**

Moon: **What cycle is the moon in?**

| Waxing Moon | Full Moon | Waning Moon | New Moon |

SELF-CARE

○ ———————————————————
○ ———————————————————
○ ———————————————————

TOP 3 PRIORITIES

○ 1: _____
○ 2: _____
○ 3: _____

ACTION STEPS

○ ———————————————————
○ ———————————————————
○ ———————————————————
○ ———————————————————
○ ———————————————————
○ ———————————————————
○ ———————————————————
○ ———————————————————
○ ———————————————————
○ ———————————————————

Daily Planner

SUN | MON | TUES | WED | THURS | FRI | SAT   DATE _____

TODAY I AM GRATEFUL FOR: _____

INNER GUIDANCE: _____

REMINDERS/NOTES: _____

Waxing Moon   Full Moon   Waning Moon   New Moon

12pm
11am   1pm
10am   2pm
9am   3pm
8am   4pm
7am   5pm
6am   6pm
5am   7pm
4am   8pm
3am   9pm
2am   10pm
1am   11pm
12am

Daily Planner

SUN | MON | TUES | WED | THURS | FRI | SAT   DATE _____

TODAY I AM GRATEFUL FOR: _____

INNER GUIDANCE: _____

REMINDERS/NOTES: _____

Waxing Moon   Full Moon   Waning Moon   New Moon

12pm
11am
10am
9am
8am
7am
6am
5am
4am
3am
2am
1am
12am
11pm
10pm
9pm
8pm
7pm
6pm
5pm
4pm
3pm
2pm
1pm

Daily Planner

SUN | MON | TUES | WED | THURS | FRI | SAT   DATE _____

TODAY I AM GRATEFUL FOR: _____

INNER GUIDANCE: _____

REMINDERS/NOTES: _____

| Waxing Moon | Full Moon | Waning Moon | New Moon |

12pm
11am   1pm
10am   2pm
9am   3pm
8am   4pm
7am   5pm
6am   6pm
5am   7pm
4am   8pm
3am   9pm
2am   10pm
1am   12am   11pm

Daily Planner

SUN | MON | TUES | WED | THURS | FRI | SAT   DATE _____

TODAY I AM GRATEFUL FOR: _____

INNER GUIDANCE: _____

REMINDERS/NOTES: _____

Waxing Moon   Full Moon   Waning Moon   New Moon

12pm
11am   1pm
10am   2pm
9am   3pm
8am   4pm
7am   5pm
6am   6pm
5am   7pm
4am   8pm
3am   9pm
2am   10pm
1am   11pm
12am

Daily Planner

SUN | MON | TUES | WED | THURS | FRI | SAT   DATE _____

TODAY I AM GRATEFUL FOR: _____

INNER GUIDANCE: _____

REMINDERS/NOTES: _____

Waxing Moon   Full Moon   Waning Moon   New Moon

12pm
11am   1pm
10am   2pm
9am   3pm
8am   4pm
7am   5pm
6am   6pm
5am   7pm
4am   8pm
3am   9pm
2am   10pm
1am   12am   11pm

Daily Planner

SUN | MON | TUES | WED | THURS | FRI | SAT   DATE _____

TODAY I AM GRATEFUL FOR: _____

INNER GUIDANCE: _____

REMINDERS/NOTES: _____

| Waxing Moon | Full Moon | Waning Moon | New Moon |

12pm
11am   1pm
10am   2pm
9am   3pm
8am   4pm
7am   5pm
6am   6pm
5am   7pm
4am   8pm
3am   9pm
2am   10pm
1am 12am 11pm

Daily Planner

SUN | MON | TUES | WED | THURS | FRI | SAT   DATE _____

TODAY I AM GRATEFUL FOR: _____

INNER GUIDANCE: _____

REMINDERS/NOTES: _____

Waxing Moon   Full Moon   Waning Moon   New Moon

12pm
11am   1pm
10am   2pm
9am   3pm
8am   4pm
7am   5pm
6am   6pm
5am   7pm
4am   8pm
3am   9pm
2am   10pm
1am   12am   11pm

Notes

_____

_____

_____

_____

_____

_____

_____

_____

_____

_____

_____

_____

_____

_____

_____

_____

_____

To order your next Fall in Love With Your Life Seasonal Planner visit: emilymadill.com

Weekly Snapshot

WEEK OF: _____

WEEKLY INTENTION/ POWER WORD: [   ]

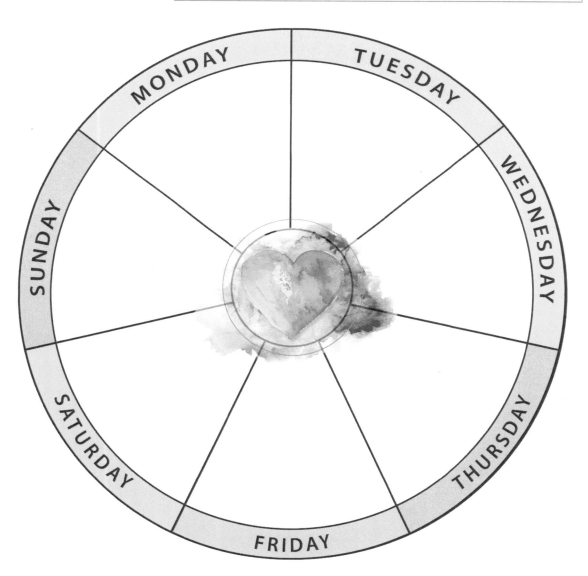

Weekly Snapshot

How will you Fall in Love With Your Life *this* week?

Heart: **How do I want to feel?**

Body: **How will I nurture my energy, health?**

Alignment: **How do I want to show up?**

Contribution: **What will I give?**

Connection: **With whom? How?**

Moon: **What cycle is the moon in?**

Waxing Moon   Full Moon   Waning Moon   New Moon

SELF-CARE

○ _____

○ _____

○ _____

TOP 3 PRIORITIES

○ 1: _____

○ 2: _____

○ 3: _____

ACTION STEPS

○ _____

○ _____

○ _____

○ _____

○ _____

○ _____

○ _____

○ _____

○ _____

○ _____

Daily Planner

SUN | MON | TUES | WED | THURS | FRI | SAT   DATE _____

TODAY I AM GRATEFUL FOR: _____

INNER GUIDANCE: _____

REMINDERS/NOTES: _____

Waxing Moon | Full Moon | Waning Moon | New Moon

12pm
11am   1pm
10am   2pm
9am   3pm
8am   4pm
7am   5pm
6am   6pm
5am   7pm
4am   8pm
3am   9pm
2am   10pm
1am   12am   11pm

Daily Planner

SUN | MON | TUES | WED | THURS | FRI | SAT   DATE _____

TODAY I AM GRATEFUL FOR: _____

INNER GUIDANCE: _____

REMINDERS/NOTES: _____

Waxing Moon   Full Moon   Waning Moon   New Moon

12pm
11am
10am
9am
8am
7am
6am
5am
4am
3am
2am
1am
12am
11pm
10pm
9pm
8pm
7pm
6pm
5pm
4pm
3pm
2pm
1pm

Daily Planner

SUN | MON | TUES | WED | THURS | FRI | SAT   DATE _____

TODAY I AM GRATEFUL FOR: _____

INNER GUIDANCE: _____

REMINDERS/NOTES: _____

Waxing Moon   Full Moon   Waning Moon   New Moon

12pm
11am   1pm
10am   2pm
9am   3pm
8am   4pm
7am   5pm
6am   6pm
5am   7pm
4am   8pm
3am   9pm
2am   10pm
1am   12am   11pm

Daily Planner

SUN | MON | TUES | WED | THURS | FRI | SAT   DATE _____

TODAY I AM GRATEFUL FOR: _____

INNER GUIDANCE: _____

REMINDERS/NOTES: _____

Waxing Moon   Full Moon   Waning Moon   New Moon

12pm
11am   1pm
10am   2pm
9am   3pm
8am   4pm
7am   5pm
6am   6pm
5am   7pm
4am   8pm
3am   9pm
2am   10pm
1am   12am   11pm

Daily Planner

SUN | MON | TUES | WED | THURS | FRI | SAT   DATE _____

TODAY I AM GRATEFUL FOR: _____

INNER GUIDANCE: _____

REMINDERS/NOTES: _____

Waxing Moon   Full Moon   Waning Moon   New Moon

12pm
11am   1pm
10am   2pm
9am   3pm
8am   4pm
7am   5pm
6am   6pm
5am   7pm
4am   8pm
3am   9pm
2am   10pm
1am   12am   11pm

Daily Planner

SUN | MON | TUES | WED | THURS | FRI | SAT   DATE _____

TODAY I AM GRATEFUL FOR: _____

INNER GUIDANCE: _____

REMINDERS/NOTES: _____

Waxing Moon   Full Moon   Waning Moon   New Moon

12pm
11am   1pm
10am   2pm
9am   3pm
8am   4pm
7am   5pm
6am   6pm
5am   7pm
4am   8pm
3am   9pm
2am   10pm
1am   12am   11pm

Daily Planner

TODAY I AM GRATEFUL FOR: _____

INNER GUIDANCE: _____

REMINDERS/NOTES: _____

Waxing
Moon

Full
Moon

Waning
Moon

New
Moon

12pm
11am   1pm
10am   2pm
9am   3pm
8am   4pm
7am   5pm
6am   6pm
5am   7pm
4am   8pm
3am   9pm
2am   10pm
1am   12am   11pm

Notes

_____

_____

_____

_____

_____

_____

_____

_____

_____

_____

_____

_____

_____

_____

_____

_____

To order your next Fall in Love With Your Life Seasonal Planner visit: emilymadill.com

Weekly Snapshot

WEEK OF: _____

WEEKLY INTENTION/
POWER WORD: [   ]

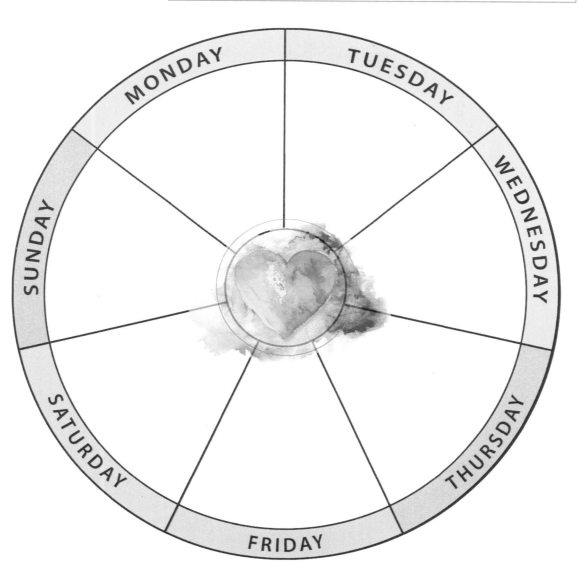

MONDAY
TUESDAY
WEDNESDAY
THURSDAY
FRIDAY
SATURDAY
SUNDAY

Weekly Snapshot

How will you Fall in Love With Your Life *this* week?

Heart: How do I want to feel?

Body: How will I nurture my energy, health?

Alignment: How do I want to show up?

Contribution: What will I give?

Connection: With whom? How?

Moon: What cycle is the moon in?

Waxing Moon   Full Moon   Waning Moon   New Moon

SELF-CARE

○ _____

○ _____

○ _____

TOP 3 PRIORITIES

○ 1: _____

○ 2: _____

○ 3: _____

ACTION STEPS

○ _____

○ _____

○ _____

○ _____

○ _____

○ _____

○ _____

○ _____

○ _____

○ _____

○ _____

Daily Planner

SUN | MON | TUES | WED | THURS | FRI | SAT   DATE _____

TODAY I AM GRATEFUL FOR: _____

INNER GUIDANCE: _____

REMINDERS/NOTES: _____

Waxing Moon   Full Moon   Waning Moon   New Moon

12pm
11am   1pm
10am   2pm
9am   3pm
8am   4pm
7am   5pm
6am   6pm
5am   7pm
4am   8pm
3am   9pm
2am   10pm
1am   12am   11pm

©Emily Madill Enterprises Ltd.

Daily Planner

SUN | MON | TUES | WED | THURS | FRI | SAT   DATE _____

TODAY I AM GRATEFUL FOR: _____

INNER GUIDANCE: _____

REMINDERS/NOTES: _____

Waxing Moon   Full Moon   Waning Moon   New Moon

12pm
11am 1pm
10am 2pm
9am 3pm
8am 4pm
7am 5pm
6am 6pm
5am 7pm
4am 8pm
3am 9pm
2am 10pm
1am 12am 11pm

Daily Planner

SUN | MON | TUES | WED | THURS | FRI | SAT   DATE _____

TODAY I AM GRATEFUL FOR: _____

INNER GUIDANCE: _____

REMINDERS/NOTES: _____

Waxing Moon   Full Moon   Waning Moon   New Moon

12pm
11am   1pm
10am   2pm
9am   3pm
8am   4pm
7am   5pm
6am   6pm
5am   7pm
4am   8pm
3am   9pm
2am   10pm
1am   12am   11pm

Daily Planner

SUN | MON | TUES | WED | THURS | FRI | SAT   DATE _____

TODAY I AM GRATEFUL FOR: _____

INNER GUIDANCE: _____

REMINDERS/NOTES: _____

Waxing Moon   Full Moon   Waning Moon   New Moon

12pm
11am
10am
9am
8am
7am
6am
5am
4am
3am
2am
1am
12am
11pm
10pm
9pm
8pm
7pm
6pm
5pm
4pm
3pm
2pm
1pm

Daily Planner

SUN | MON | TUES | WED | THURS | FRI | SAT   DATE _____

TODAY I AM GRATEFUL FOR: _____

INNER GUIDANCE: _____

REMINDERS/NOTES: _____

Waxing Moon   Full Moon   Waning Moon   New Moon

12pm
11am   1pm
10am   2pm
9am   3pm
8am   4pm
7am   5pm
6am   6pm
5am   7pm
4am   8pm
3am   9pm
2am   10pm
1am   12am   11pm

Daily Planner

SUN | MON | TUES | WED | THURS | FRI | SAT   DATE _____

TODAY I AM GRATEFUL FOR: _____

INNER GUIDANCE: _____

REMINDERS/NOTES: _____

Waxing Moon   Full Moon   Waning Moon   New Moon

12pm
11am
1pm
10am
2pm
9am
3pm
8am
4pm
7am
5pm
6am
6pm
5am
7pm
4am
8pm
3am
9pm
2am
10pm
1am
12am
11pm

Daily Planner

SUN | MON | TUES | WED | THURS | FRI | SAT   DATE _____

TODAY I AM GRATEFUL FOR: _____

INNER GUIDANCE: _____

REMINDERS/NOTES: _____

Waxing Moon   Full Moon   Waning Moon   New Moon

12pm
11am
1pm
10am
2pm
9am
3pm
8am
4pm
7am
5pm
6am
6pm
5am
7pm
4am
8pm
3am
9pm
2am
10pm
1am
12am
11pm

Notes

_____

_____

_____

_____

_____

_____

_____

_____

_____

_____

_____

_____

_____

_____

_____

To order your next Fall in Love With Your Life Seasonal Planner visit: emilymadill.com

Weekly Snapshot

WEEK OF: _____

WEEKLY INTENTION/
POWER WORD: [   ]

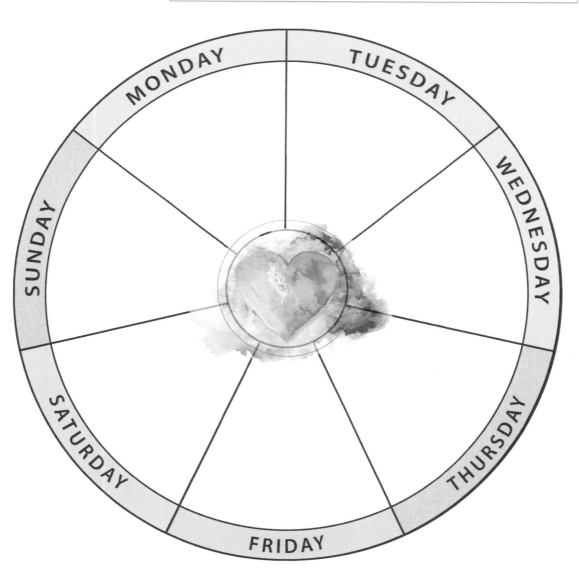

Weekly Snapshot

How will you Fall in Love With Your Life *this* week?

Heart: **How do I want to feel?**

Body: **How will I nurture my energy, health?**

Alignment: **How do I want to show up?**

Contribution: **What will I give?**

Connection: **With whom? How?**

Moon: **What cycle is the moon in?**

Waxing Moon   Full Moon   Waning Moon   New Moon

SELF-CARE

○ _____
○ _____
○ _____

TOP 3 PRIORITIES

○ 1: _____
○ 2: _____
○ 3: _____

ACTION STEPS

○ _____
○ _____
○ _____
○ _____
○ _____
○ _____
○ _____
○ _____
○ _____
○ _____

Daily Planner

SUN | MON | TUES | WED | THURS | FRI | SAT   DATE _____

TODAY I AM GRATEFUL FOR: _____

INNER GUIDANCE: _____

REMINDERS/NOTES: _____

Waxing Moon   Full Moon   Waning Moon   New Moon

12pm
11am   1pm
10am   2pm
9am   3pm
8am   4pm
7am   5pm
6am   6pm
5am   7pm
4am   8pm
3am   9pm
2am   10pm
1am   12am   11pm

Daily Planner

SUN | MON | TUES | WED | THURS | FRI | SAT   DATE _____

TODAY I AM GRATEFUL FOR: _____

INNER GUIDANCE: _____

REMINDERS/NOTES: _____

| Waxing Moon | Full Moon | Waning Moon | New Moon |

12pm
11am
10am
9am
8am
7am
6am
5am
4am
3am
2am
1am
12am
11pm
10pm
9pm
8pm
7pm
6pm
5pm
4pm
3pm
2pm
1pm

Daily Planner

SUN | MON | TUES | WED | THURS | FRI | SAT   DATE _____

TODAY I AM GRATEFUL FOR: _____

INNER GUIDANCE: _____

REMINDERS/NOTES: _____

Waxing Moon   Full Moon   Waning Moon   New Moon

12pm
11am   1pm
10am   2pm
9am   3pm
8am   4pm
7am   5pm
6am   6pm
5am   7pm
4am   8pm
3am   9pm
2am   10pm
1am   12am   11pm

Daily Planner

SUN | MON | TUES | WED | THURS | FRI | SAT   DATE _____

TODAY I AM GRATEFUL FOR: _____

INNER GUIDANCE: _____

REMINDERS/NOTES: _____

Waxing Moon   Full Moon   Waning Moon   New Moon

12pm
11am
1pm
10am
2pm
9am
3pm
8am
4pm
7am
5pm
6am
6pm
5am
7pm
4am
8pm
3am
9pm
2am
10pm
1am
12am
11pm

Daily Planner

SUN | MON | TUES | WED | THURS | FRI | SAT   DATE _____

TODAY I AM GRATEFUL FOR: _____

INNER GUIDANCE: _____

REMINDERS/NOTES: _____

Waxing Moon   Full Moon   Waning Moon   New Moon

12pm
11am
1pm
10am
2pm
9am
3pm
8am
4pm
7am
5pm
6am
6pm
5am
7pm
4am
8pm
3am
9pm
2am
10pm
1am
12am
11pm

Daily Planner

SUN | MON | TUES | WED | THURS | FRI | SAT   DATE _____

TODAY I AM GRATEFUL FOR: _____

INNER GUIDANCE: _____

REMINDERS/NOTES: _____

Waxing Moon   Full Moon   Waning Moon   New Moon

12pm
11am
1pm
10am
2pm
9am
3pm
8am
4pm
7am
5pm
6am
6pm
5am
7pm
4am
8pm
3am
9pm
2am
10pm
1am
12am
11pm

Daily Planner

SUN | MON | TUES | WED | THURS | FRI | SAT   DATE _____

TODAY I AM GRATEFUL FOR: _____

INNER GUIDANCE: _____

REMINDERS/NOTES: _____

Waxing Moon   Full Moon   Waning Moon   New Moon

12pm
11am
1pm
10am
2pm
9am
3pm
8am
4pm
7am
5pm
6am
6pm
5am
7pm
4am
8pm
3am
9pm
2am
10pm
1am
12am
11pm

Notes

_____

_____

_____

_____

_____

_____

_____

_____

_____

_____

_____

_____

_____

_____

To order your next Fall in Love With Your Life Seasonal Planner visit: emilymadill.com

Weekly Snapshot

WEEK OF: _____

WEEKLY INTENTION/ POWER WORD: [   ]

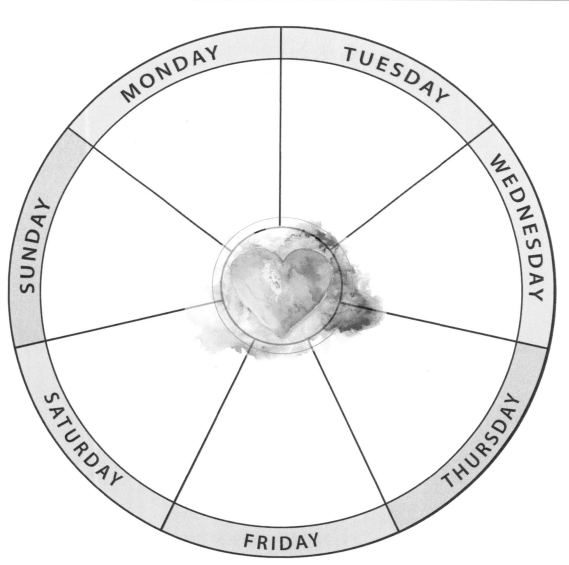

Weekly Snapshot

How will you Fall in Love With Your Life *this* week?

Heart: **How do I want to feel?**

Body: **How will I nurture my energy, health?**

Alignment: **How do I want to show up?**

Contribution: **What will I give?**

Connection: **With whom? How?**

Moon: **What cycle is the moon in?**

Waxing Moon   Full Moon   Waning Moon   New Moon

SELF-CARE

○ —————————————————
○ —————————————————
○ —————————————————

TOP 3 PRIORITIES

○ 1: _____
○ 2: _____
○ 3: _____

ACTION STEPS

○ —————————————————
○ —————————————————
○ —————————————————
○ —————————————————
○ —————————————————
○ —————————————————
○ —————————————————
○ —————————————————
○ —————————————————
○ —————————————————

Daily Planner

SUN | MON | TUES | WED | THURS | FRI | SAT   DATE _____

TODAY I AM GRATEFUL FOR: _____

INNER GUIDANCE: _____

REMINDERS/NOTES: _____

Waxing Moon   Full Moon   Waning Moon   New Moon

12pm
11am   1pm
10am   2pm
9am   3pm
8am   4pm
7am   5pm
6am   6pm
5am   7pm
4am   8pm
3am   9pm
2am   10pm
1am   12am   11pm

Daily Planner

TODAY I AM GRATEFUL FOR: _____

INNER GUIDANCE: _____

REMINDERS/NOTES: _____

Waxing Moon   Full Moon   Waning Moon   New Moon

12pm
11am   1pm
10am   2pm
9am   3pm
8am   4pm
7am   5pm
6am   6pm
5am   7pm
4am   8pm
3am   9pm
2am   10pm
1am   12am   11pm

Daily Planner

SUN | MON | TUES | WED | THURS | FRI | SAT   DATE _____

TODAY I AM GRATEFUL FOR: _____

INNER GUIDANCE: _____

REMINDERS/NOTES: _____

Waxing Moon   Full Moon   Waning Moon   New Moon

12pm
11am   1pm
10am   2pm
9am   3pm
8am   4pm
7am   5pm
6am   6pm
5am   7pm
4am   8pm
3am   9pm
2am   10pm
1am   12am   11pm

Daily Planner

SUN | MON | TUES | WED | THURS | FRI | SAT   DATE _____

TODAY I AM GRATEFUL FOR: _____

INNER GUIDANCE: _____

REMINDERS/NOTES: _____

Waxing Moon	Full Moon	Waning Moon	New Moon

12pm
11am
10am
9am
8am
7am
6am
5am
4am
3am
2am
1am
12am
11pm
10pm
9pm
8pm
7pm
6pm
5pm
4pm
3pm
2pm
1pm

Daily Planner

SUN | MON | TUES | WED | THURS | FRI | SAT   DATE _____

TODAY I AM GRATEFUL FOR: _____

INNER GUIDANCE: _____

REMINDERS/NOTES: _____

Waxing Moon   Full Moon   Waning Moon   New Moon

12pm
11am   1pm
10am   2pm
9am   3pm
8am   4pm
7am   5pm
6am   6pm
5am   7pm
4am   8pm
3am   9pm
2am   10pm
1am   12am   11pm

Daily Planner

SUN | MON | TUES | WED | THURS | FRI | SAT   DATE _____

TODAY I AM GRATEFUL FOR: _____

INNER GUIDANCE: _____

REMINDERS/NOTES: _____

Waxing Moon   Full Moon   Waning Moon   New Moon

12pm
11am   1pm
10am   2pm
9am   3pm
8am   4pm
7am   5pm
6am   6pm
5am   7pm
4am   8pm
3am   9pm
2am   10pm
1am   12am   11pm

Daily Planner

SUN | MON | TUES | WED | THURS | FRI | SAT   DATE _____

TODAY I AM GRATEFUL FOR: _____

INNER GUIDANCE: _____

REMINDERS/NOTES: _____

Waxing Moon   Full Moon   Waning Moon   New Moon

12pm
11am   1pm
10am   2pm
9am   3pm
8am   4pm
7am   5pm
6am   6pm
5am   7pm
4am   8pm
3am   9pm
2am   10pm
1am   12am   11pm

Notes

_____

_____

_____

_____

_____

_____

_____

_____

_____

_____

_____

_____

_____

_____

_____

Weekly Snapshot

WEEK OF: _____

WEEKLY INTENTION/ POWER WORD:

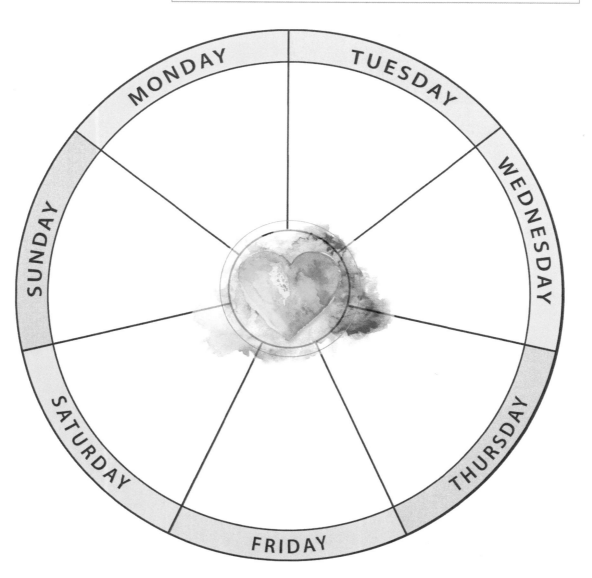

Weekly Snapshot

How will you Fall in Love With Your Life *this* week?

Heart: **How do I want to feel?**

Body: **How will I nurture my energy, health?**

Alignment: **How do I want to show up?**

Contribution: **What will I give?**

Connection: **With whom? How?**

Moon: **What cycle is the moon in?**

Waxing Moon   Full Moon   Waning Moon   New Moon

SELF-CARE

○ _____

○ _____

○ _____

TOP 3 PRIORITIES

○ 1: _____

○ 2: _____

○ 3: _____

ACTION STEPS

○ _____

○ _____

○ _____

○ _____

○ _____

○ _____

○ _____

○ _____

○ _____

○ _____

Daily Planner

SUN | MON | TUES | WED | THURS | FRI | SAT   DATE _____

TODAY I AM GRATEFUL FOR: _____

INNER GUIDANCE: _____

REMINDERS/NOTES: _____

| Waxing Moon | Full Moon | Waning Moon | New Moon |

12pm
11am   1pm
10am   2pm
9am   3pm
8am   4pm
7am   5pm
6am   6pm
5am   7pm
4am   8pm
3am   9pm
2am   10pm
1am   12am   11pm

Daily Planner

SUN | MON | TUES | WED | THURS | FRI | SAT   DATE _____

TODAY I AM GRATEFUL FOR: _____

INNER GUIDANCE: _____

REMINDERS/NOTES: _____

Waxing Moon   Full Moon   Waning Moon   New Moon

12pm
11am   1pm
10am   2pm
9am   3pm
8am   4pm
7am   5pm
6am   6pm
5am   7pm
4am   8pm
3am   9pm
2am   10pm
1am   12am   11pm

Daily Planner

TODAY I AM GRATEFUL FOR: _____

INNER GUIDANCE: _____

REMINDERS/NOTES: _____

Waxing Moon   Full Moon   Waning Moon   New Moon

12pm
11am   1pm
10am   2pm
9am   3pm
8am   4pm
7am   5pm
6am   6pm
5am   7pm
4am   8pm
3am   9pm
2am   10pm
1am   12am   11pm

Daily Planner

SUN | MON | TUES | WED | THURS | FRI | SAT   DATE _____

TODAY I AM GRATEFUL FOR: _____

INNER GUIDANCE: _____

REMINDERS/NOTES: _____

Waxing Moon   Full Moon   Waning Moon   New Moon

12pm
11am   1pm
10am   2pm
9am   3pm
8am   4pm
7am   5pm
6am   6pm
5am   7pm
4am   8pm
3am   9pm
2am   10pm
1am 12am 11pm

Daily Planner

SUN | MON | TUES | WED | THURS | FRI | SAT   DATE _____

TODAY I AM GRATEFUL FOR: _____

INNER GUIDANCE: _____

REMINDERS/NOTES: _____

Waxing Moon   Full Moon   Waning Moon   New Moon

12pm
11am
1pm
10am
2pm
9am
3pm
8am
4pm
7am
5pm
6am
6pm
5am
7pm
4am
8pm
3am
9pm
2am
10pm
1am
12am
11pm

Daily Planner

SUN | MON | TUES | WED | THURS | FRI | SAT   DATE _____

TODAY I AM GRATEFUL FOR: _____

INNER GUIDANCE: _____

REMINDERS/NOTES: _____

Waxing Moon   Full Moon   Waning Moon   New Moon

12pm
11am
1pm
10am
2pm
9am
3pm
8am
4pm
7am
5pm
6am
6pm
5am
7pm
4am
8pm
3am
9pm
2am
10pm
1am
12am
11pm

Daily Planner

SUN | MON | TUES | WED | THURS | FRI | SAT   DATE _____

TODAY I AM GRATEFUL FOR: _____

INNER GUIDANCE: _____

REMINDERS/NOTES: _____

Waxing Moon   Full Moon   Waning Moon   New Moon

12pm
11am   1pm
10am   2pm
9am   3pm
8am   4pm
7am   5pm
6am   6pm
5am   7pm
4am   8pm
3am   9pm
2am   10pm
1am   12am   11pm

Notes

_____

_____

_____

_____

_____

_____

_____

_____

_____

_____

_____

_____

_____

_____

_____

To order your next Fall in Love With Your Life Seasonal Planner visit: emilymadill.com

Weekly Snapshot

WEEK OF: _____

WEEKLY INTENTION/
POWER WORD:

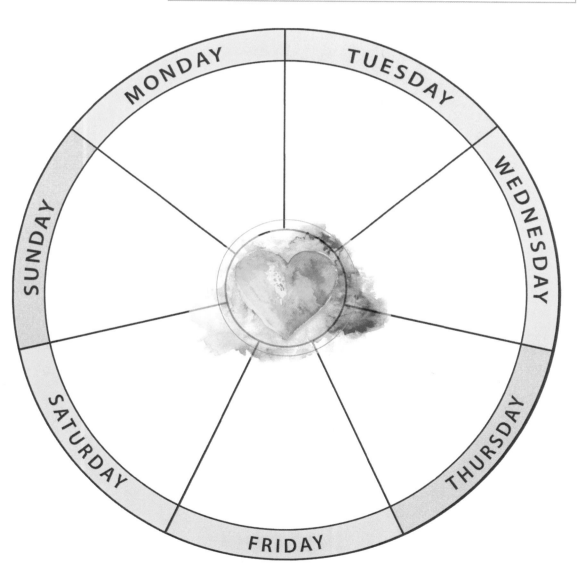

Weekly Snapshot

How will you Fall in Love With Your Life *this* week?

Heart: How do I want to feel?

Body: How will I nurture my energy, health?

Alignment: How do I want to show up?

Contribution: What will I give?

Connection: With whom? How?

Moon: What cycle is the moon in?

Waxing Moon   Full Moon   Waning Moon   New Moon

SELF-CARE

○ _____
○ _____
○ _____

TOP 3 PRIORITIES

○ 1: _____
○ 2: _____
○ 3: _____

ACTION STEPS

○ _____
○ _____
○ _____
○ _____
○ _____
○ _____
○ _____
○ _____
○ _____
○ _____

Daily Planner

SUN | MON | TUES | WED | THURS | FRI | SAT   DATE _____

TODAY I AM GRATEFUL FOR: _____

INNER GUIDANCE: _____

REMINDERS/NOTES: _____

Waxing Moon   Full Moon   Waning Moon   New Moon

12pm
11am 1pm
10am 2pm
9am 3pm
8am 4pm
7am 5pm
6am 6pm
5am 7pm
4am 8pm
3am 9pm
2am 10pm
1am 12am 11pm

Daily Planner

SUN | MON | TUES | WED | THURS | FRI | SAT   DATE _____

TODAY I AM GRATEFUL FOR: _____

INNER GUIDANCE: _____

REMINDERS/NOTES: _____

Waxing Moon   Full Moon   Waning Moon   New Moon

12pm
11am
1pm
10am
2pm
9am
3pm
8am
4pm
7am
5pm
6am
6pm
5am
7pm
4am
8pm
3am
9pm
2am
10pm
1am
12am
11pm

Daily Planner

SUN | MON | TUES | WED | THURS | FRI | SAT   DATE _____

TODAY I AM GRATEFUL FOR: _____

INNER GUIDANCE: _____

REMINDERS/NOTES: _____

Waxing Moon   Full Moon   Waning Moon   New Moon

12pm
11am   1pm
10am   2pm
9am   3pm
8am   4pm
7am   5pm
6am   6pm
5am   7pm
4am   8pm
3am   9pm
2am   10pm
1am   12am   11pm

Daily Planner

SUN | MON | TUES | WED | THURS | FRI | SAT   DATE _____

TODAY I AM GRATEFUL FOR: _____

INNER GUIDANCE: _____

REMINDERS/NOTES: _____

Waxing Moon   Full Moon   Waning Moon   New Moon

12pm
11am
10am
9am
8am
7am
6am
5am
4am
3am
2am
1am
12am
11pm
10pm
9pm
8pm
7pm
6pm
5pm
4pm
3pm
2pm
1pm

Daily Planner

SUN | MON | TUES | WED | THURS | FRI | SAT   DATE _____

TODAY I AM GRATEFUL FOR: _____

INNER GUIDANCE: _____

REMINDERS/NOTES: _____

Waxing
Moon   Full
Moon   Waning
Moon   New
Moon

12pm
11am   1pm
10am   2pm
9am   3pm
8am   4pm
7am   5pm
6am   6pm
5am   7pm
4am   8pm
3am   9pm
2am   10pm
1am   12am   11pm

Daily Planner

SUN | MON | TUES | WED | THURS | FRI | SAT   DATE _____

TODAY I AM GRATEFUL FOR: _____

INNER GUIDANCE: _____

REMINDERS/NOTES: _____

Waxing Moon   Full Moon   Waning Moon   New Moon

12pm
11am   1pm
10am   2pm
9am   3pm
8am   4pm
7am   5pm
6am   6pm
5am   7pm
4am   8pm
3am   9pm
2am   10pm
1am   12am   11pm

Daily Planner

SUN | MON | TUES | WED | THURS | FRI | SAT   DATE _____

TODAY I AM GRATEFUL FOR: _____

INNER GUIDANCE: _____

REMINDERS/NOTES: _____

Waxing Moon   Full Moon   Waning Moon   New Moon

12pm
11am   1pm
10am   2pm
9am   3pm
8am   4pm
7am   5pm
6am   6pm
5am   7pm
4am   8pm
3am   9pm
2am   10pm
1am   12am   11pm

Notes

_____

_____

_____

_____

_____

_____

_____

_____

_____

_____

_____

_____

_____

_____

To order your next Fall in Love With Your Life Seasonal Planner visit: emilymadill.com

Weekly Snapshot

WEEK OF: _____

**WEEKLY INTENTION/
POWER WORD:** [   ]

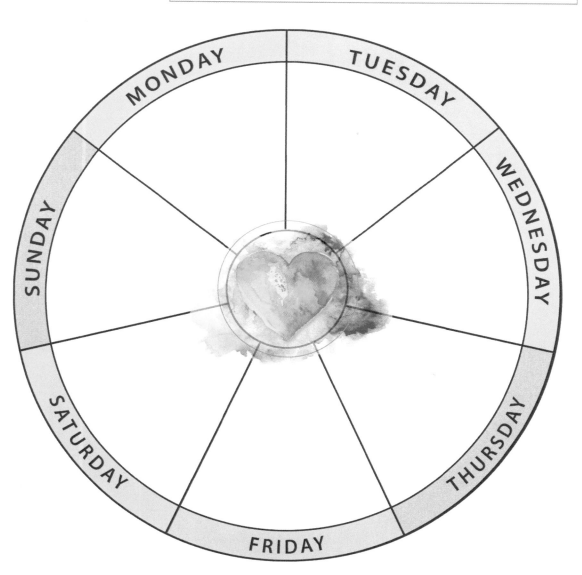

MONDAY · TUESDAY · WEDNESDAY · THURSDAY · FRIDAY · SATURDAY · SUNDAY

Weekly Snapshot

How will you Fall in Love With Your Life *this* week?

Heart: How do I want to feel?

Body: How will I nurture my energy, health?

Alignment: How do I want to show up?

Contribution: What will I give?

Connection: With whom? How?

Moon: What cycle is the moon in?

Waxing Moon   Full Moon   Waning Moon   New Moon

SELF-CARE

○ _____

○ _____

○ _____

TOP 3 PRIORITIES

○ 1: _____

○ 2: _____

○ 3: _____

ACTION STEPS

○ _____

○ _____

○ _____

○ _____

○ _____

○ _____

○ _____

○ _____

○ _____

○ _____

○ _____

Daily Planner

SUN | MON | TUES | WED | THURS | FRI | SAT   DATE _____

TODAY I AM GRATEFUL FOR: _____

INNER GUIDANCE: _____

REMINDERS/NOTES: _____

Waxing Moon   Full Moon   Waning Moon   New Moon

12pm
11am   1pm
10am   2pm
9am   3pm
8am   4pm
7am   5pm
6am   6pm
5am   7pm
4am   8pm
3am   9pm
2am   10pm
1am 12am 11pm

Daily Planner

SUN | MON | TUES | WED | THURS | FRI | SAT   DATE _____

TODAY I AM GRATEFUL FOR: _____

INNER GUIDANCE: _____

REMINDERS/NOTES: _____

Waxing Moon   Full Moon   Waning Moon   New Moon

12pm
11am   1pm
10am   2pm
9am   3pm
8am   4pm
7am   5pm
6am   6pm
5am   7pm
4am   8pm
3am   9pm
2am   10pm
1am   12am   11pm

Daily Planner

SUN | MON | TUES | WED | THURS | FRI | SAT   DATE _____

TODAY I AM GRATEFUL FOR: _____

INNER GUIDANCE: _____

REMINDERS/NOTES: _____

Waxing Moon   Full Moon   Waning Moon   New Moon

12pm
11am   1pm
10am   2pm
9am   3pm
8am   4pm
7am   5pm
6am   6pm
5am   7pm
4am   8pm
3am   9pm
2am   10pm
1am   12am   11pm

Daily Planner

SUN | MON | TUES | WED | THURS | FRI | SAT   DATE _____

TODAY I AM GRATEFUL FOR: _____

INNER GUIDANCE: _____

REMINDERS/NOTES: _____

Waxing Moon   Full Moon   Waning Moon   New Moon

12pm
11am   1pm
10am   2pm
9am   3pm
8am   4pm
7am   5pm
6am   6pm
5am   7pm
4am   8pm
3am   9pm
2am   10pm
1am   12am   11pm

Daily Planner

SUN | MON | TUES | WED | THURS | FRI | SAT   DATE _____

TODAY I AM GRATEFUL FOR: _____

INNER GUIDANCE: _____

REMINDERS/NOTES: _____

Waxing Moon | Full Moon | Waning Moon | New Moon

12pm
11am   1pm
10am   2pm
9am   3pm
8am   4pm
7am   5pm
6am   6pm
5am   7pm
4am   8pm
3am   9pm
2am   10pm
1am   12am   11pm

Daily Planner

SUN | MON | TUES | WED | THURS | FRI | SAT   DATE _____

TODAY I AM GRATEFUL FOR: _____

INNER GUIDANCE: _____

REMINDERS/NOTES: _____

Waxing Moon   Full Moon   Waning Moon   New Moon

12pm
11am   1pm
10am   2pm
9am   3pm
8am   4pm
7am   5pm
6am   6pm
5am   7pm
4am   8pm
3am   9pm
2am   10pm
1am   12am   11pm

Daily Planner

SUN | MON | TUES | WED | THURS | FRI | SAT   DATE _____

TODAY I AM GRATEFUL FOR: _____

INNER GUIDANCE: _____

REMINDERS/NOTES: _____

Waxing Moon   Full Moon   Waning Moon   New Moon

12pm
11am   1pm
10am   2pm
9am   3pm
8am   4pm
7am   5pm
6am   6pm
5am   7pm
4am   8pm
3am   9pm
2am   10pm
1am   12am   11pm

Notes

_____

_____

_____

_____

_____

_____

_____

_____

_____

_____

_____

_____

_____

_____

_____

To order your next Fall in Love With Your Life Seasonal Planner visit: emilymadill.com

Start fresh when you feel stuck

Sometimes life is all smooth sailing, and other times it can feel like we're navigating through thick mud. During difficult times we might wonder: *How did I end up here? Why does it all feel so hard? Will I ever get that break?*

When we end up in stuck places, it's challenging to know how to get back to calm waters. It's hard to see how we will regain our sense that all is well. The challenges feel hard and draining and we can feel stuck without an end in sight.

Getting to that other side in our personal life, professional life or our overall sense of joy for life – can feel out of reach.

I get it, I've been there (more than once) in all areas of life. Catching that lucky break can feel like a roller coaster of a waiting game. Waiting for something external to shift before we experience relief only amplifies feeling stuck and disempowered.

Over time, I've learned if I still feel stuck in the mud after putting in my best effort, it's a sign to turn the page and start fresh.

Turning the page can be helpful with big obstacles in life and it can also bring relief to the small day to day jams we get caught up in.

Turning the page is surrendering to what is hard. It's saying, I don't know what to do with this storm I'm in, so I'm going to turn the page and start fresh.

When we've stayed in the agony long enough, it's about saying enough is enough. I can't change what is, but I can see life before me with new perspective. I can begin a new chapter – one that isn't bogged down by my current frame of reality.

Here are the three strategies I use to move through stuck places and turn the page to begin fresh.

1. Start where you are

Think: Presence and gratitude.

When we feel stuck, starting with where we are might seem like a lost cause – after all we feel stuck! But, starting with where we are is really about presence and gratitude. We can shelf the story about our current circumstances, and instead bring to mind all the things (I mean all the things) we are grateful for.

List them out loud, on paper, to yourself or to a loved one. Create new energy around what is good about life. Consider everything that is before you in this moment.

What can you see, hear, smell, taste and touch?

If it's helpful, keep it basic to bring your awareness to a level that's in sync with the moment you're in. Then allow your mind to expand out to the more detailed and abstract reasons why life is good.

Allow it all to sink in. Marvel in the magic of your surroundings and notice how this complicated and beautiful thing called life is actually a gift.

Turning the page isn't about ignoring or denying truths. It's about choosing to not become swallowed by them. We are all participants in life. How we choose to participate in our own unique life journey is our superpower.

It's easier to shift our mindset when we start with where we are right now in this moment. Simply focus on gratitude.

2. Self-Reflection

Think: Strong connected relationship with yourself and your truth.

Our perception of our outer world is a reflection of our inner world. When we make a habit of checking in with ourselves on a daily basis, we become familiar with the tapestry of our inner world. Then when we feel like we are being swallowed by challenges in our external world, we can venture inward and see what might need shifting.

When searching for answers on how to unstick ourselves or be happier, our usual default is to look outside of ourselves before venturing inward.

As a society, we put too much power in the hands of our external world and not enough faith in our inner guide. We are all so incredibly resourceful. The more we check in before we look outside, the easier it is to stick on the path that feels best for

us. The easier it also becomes to move through stuck places and make steps forward in alignment with our authentic selves.

With practice, our perception of our outer world can be influenced by our inner world from a more conscious place. This is an empowering stance and one that can move us out of feeling stuck.

Building and maintaining strong relationships with ourselves begins with regular self-reflection. How we practice self-reflection is a personal preference. Some people like to journal, others practice quiet meditation. Connecting inward might come easily when you are in nature, or enjoying a favorite activity.

Perhaps, checking in with yourself is something you like to do at the start of your day, at the end of your day – maybe it's something you'll do periodically throughout the day.

Building strong relationships with other people, is the same as building one with yourself. It takes time, consistency, patience, trust, humour and loyalty – above all it takes love.

3. Train your mind to turn on a dime

Think: Choice, perspective, empowerment.

'To turn on a dime' has to do with our ability to quickly adjust and shift with what's before us, so we stay on our highest path. Our highest path considers that happiness and well-being are critical components of a life well-lived and loved.

Our perspective creates our experience of life. Our choice to adjust our perspective is our source of power. When we witness our ability to shift perspective and turn the page, we build more faith in ourselves.

These questions can fuel a shift in perspective and ease stuck places. The idea is to create a bit of space and have an honest conversation with yourself. If this process speaks to you, take your time and use these question prompts as a starting place:

- What do I want to feel?

- Why do I want to feel that? Why is that important to me now?

- What is one step I can take right now that will move me closer to my desired feeling?

- How might moving closer to my core desired feeling influence other aspects of my day?

- Then when you've taken that step, what's the next step? (remember to stay focused on what you do want, not what you don't).

These empowering questions help us course-correct to stay on our highest path. We may not choose the storms in life, but we have a say in how we weather them. You've got this.

How might turning the page change the course of your day?

For more inspiration and articles like these, visit Emily's blog/article library at:

emilymadill.com

Notes

_____

_____

_____

_____

_____

_____

_____

_____

_____

_____

_____

_____

_____

_____

_____

To order your next Fall in Love With Your Life Seasonal Planner visit: emilymadill.com

Acknowledgements

Creating this planner has been particularly important to me because I use it as a daily tool in my own life. I know it will help others create a life they love, but I couldn't have done it without the help and influence of others.

I would like to acknowledge some of them here, in no particular order, as having either influenced, inspired, taught or collaborated with me to make this *Fall in Life With Your Life Seasonal Planner* what you now hold in your hands.

My grandma taught me a lot about the ritual of recording time. At 93, she still keeps her calendar close. For most of her life, she kept a daily journal with pen to paper, uniquely capturing her own life journey. My mom has been my most influential spiritual teacher. It's through her, I have the strong belief that our greatest source of power and wisdom comes from inside ourselves. My husband Ehren has taught me that every day is meant to be the very best day of your life. He is my daily example that it's possible to fill your entire day, from start to finish, doing all of your favorite things – it comes down to attitude. My sons, Joe and Jake, remind me to prioritize what's most important and be mindful not to fill my day with things that take away from where I truly want and need to be. My entire family, on all sides, have instilled in me the value of holding close what you treasure, and to count your blessings on a daily basis. Everything is cyclical – all things eventually come to pass and that includes the journey of living.

My soul sister Angela has taught me the value of sisterhood and holding boundaries. My dear kindred spirit-friend Amanda has taught me that while it's valuable to have a container and map for your time, it's equally valuable to go with the natural rhythm and cycle of your life. My close confidant, neighbor, sister-wife and run partner Cheri reminds me it's possible and important to be on time, to make time for what's important, and to not add so many things to your plate that you feel overwhelmed. My cherished friendship with Nicole reminds me that good friends can be separated by distance, but always pick up right where we left off. My beautiful friend Kathy has taught me to never take anyone, or any moment in time for granted.

My women's groups influence me in so many ways. My *I Love Us* group of friends has taught me about the value of community and that women are incredibly resourceful and supportive. My *Chics and Cronies* family, Tasha, Adrianne and Michelle, have taught me about the value of sharing history and a bond that stands the test of time. My clever, powerhouse friend Crystal and our *Creatrix Mastermind* crew have taught me the importance of prioritizing and making time to celebrate your wins along the way. My sports family, that accompany having two boys in competitive sports,

have taught me that it's the little things that add up to a game well-played – or a life well-lived and loved.

My friend, filmmaker Nic Askew has taught me firsthand about presence and stillness and that it's possible to achieve both of those, anytime, anywhere, with anyone. Spiritual teacher Mike Dooley has taught me that thoughts do become things and having a glad heart is all that truly matters in life.

My friend Hope Koppelman reminds me that creativity is more about the journey and process, than it is about the end product or goal.

Arianna Huffington taught me about all things *microsteps*. She has also taught me about the importance of opening doors and the gift of giving opportunities. As one of Thrive Global's Editors-at-Large, I am deeply grateful for doors she has opened for me.

My coaching education through Erickson International was transformational in how I view time. It is through Erickson that I learned about the many tools I use in my coaching practice, including the Life Balance Wheel you see in this planner.

Kate Northrup has been an influential teacher in my business and how I approach time using a feminine model. I learned about viewing and approaching the day in a 24-hour circle, like you see in the daily planner, from her beautiful Origin Membership group, and her *Do Less Planner System*. Kate also led me to Marie Forleo's work through B-School. Marie has helped me see that

everyone has a valuable gift to share with the world – including me.

This planner would not be here at all, nor would it be elegant, feminine and beautiful without the collaboration with Constance Mears. Connie worked with me on all aspects of the planner from idea to final form. She was patient, kind, supportive and also gave me the nudges I needed, when I needed them. Connie is more than a teammate and creative collaborator; she is a dear friend and mentor whom I cherish.

These wonderful people have all, in their own unique ways, influenced how I view time and how I want to spend my time. I see each of them and their imprint on my life, when I flip through the pages of this planner. I hope you enjoy the collective energy that is very much alive in this *Fall in Love With Your Life Seasonal Planner*. For me, it has always been about a tool that helps to support others to believe in themselves and to live their truest version of life. It's a tool I use to help me do exactly that, one week, one micro-step at a time.

🩶 With Love,

Emily

Made in the USA
Columbia, SC
15 March 2021